RISE UP

A 40-day Journey into the Heart of God

Rise Up: A 40-day Journey into the Heart of God
Published by Catch The Fire Books
272 Attwell Drive, Toronto ON M9W 6M3 Canada

Distributed worldwide by Catch The Fire Distribution. Titles may be purchased in bulk.
For information, please contact distribution@catchthefire.com.

Catch The Fire® is a registered trademark of Catch The Fire World.

Any website addresses recommended throughout this book are offered as a resource to
you. These websites are not intended in any way to imply an endorsement on the part of
Catch The Fire, nor do we vouch for their content. The information in this book was correct
at the time it was published.

ISBN 978-1-894310-90-1
Copyright © 2016 Michael Whate

The Team: Hanna Glover, Marcott Bernarde, Benjamin Jackson, Jonathan Puddle, Steve Long
Cover design: Marcott Bernarde (Catch The Fire)
Interior layout: Medlar Publishing Solutions Pvt Ltd, India

Printed in Canada
March 2016

RISE UP

A 40-day Journey into the Heart of God

Michael Whate

Table of Contents

Introduction

My hope in writing this devotional is to help you strengthen your relationship with God, and allow you to better discover His plan and purpose for your life. I believe that it is meant for all Christians, men and women, young and old, new believer and veteran; regardless of your denomination or church background.

In preparing the content, I have deliberately avoided deep discussion on theological or doctrinal matters, rather I simply share scripture passages and relate these to my own life-story—a life that has been transformed from a somewhat nominal Christian to someone who is fully committed to and living for Christ. This journey took me from a desperate cry for help, to a place of peace and personal intimacy with God. Each daily meditation ends with a conversational prayer and an invitation for you to reflect on the message and apply it to your own life.

Throughout scripture God uses 40 days as a time of preparation, purification and sometimes, testing. For instance, rain fell on the earth 40 days and 40 nights during the great flood (Genesis 7:12). Moses was on Mount Sinai for 40 days and 40 nights receiving the covenant from the Lord (Exodus 34:28). Elijah travelled for 40 days across the desert to reach Mount Horeb, where he encountered the Lord (1 Kings 19:7). Jonah persuaded the sinful Ninevites to fast for 40 days, and thus, God relented and did not destroy their city (Jonah 3:3); and the Spirit of God led Jesus to spend 40 days fasting and praying in the desert before He began his public ministry. Since early Christian times the Roman Catholic Church has celebrated the season of Lent as a 40 day period of fasting and repentance in preparation for Easter.

With this 40 day God-pattern in mind, I invite you set out on this journey with me; you don't have to complete it in 40 days, I suggest that you take as much time as necessary and allow God to speak words of encouragement and perhaps direction into your life. You may also wish to use selected messages for small group discussion and use the Topical Index to find specific prayers and subjects as you need them. If you are looking for more information on selected topics please consult the section on "Suggestions for Further Reading". Also visit my website riseupdevotional.com where you can read or download new material, discuss with others, or purchase additional copies of this book.

In order to give you a frame of reference, allow me to share a brief introduction of my background and how this book came to be written—I will share these events in greater detail later on. I was born in London, England, shortly after the outbreak of World War II, the youngest of four children. My Mom was Roman Catholic and Dad was an Anglican. I was educated by Benedictine monks in a Catholic School; but despite this schooling my spirituality was very immature. You see, I followed all the rules of the Church but did not have a personal relationship with God. It often seemed to me that when I left the church building, God remained behind. That doesn't seem right, does it? And yet, I believe it's a common experience.

I came to Canada in 1965 and the following year I fell in love and married my wife Marion; we have since been blessed with three amazing sons Steve, Rich, and Rob. In the early 1970's, I experienced my first real face-to-face encounter with God. It occurred during a Catholic retreat weekend. It was during this retreat that I came to know Jesus not only as my Savior, but also as a real living person who loves me unconditionally. Some years later, I was drawn into the Catholic Charismatic movement where I received a "supernatural download" from the Holy Spirit—my own personal Pentecost experience. This proved to be a turning point in my life—as I gained a new love and appreciation for the Bible and became active in my church and in the Healing Ministry. Later, in the late 1990's, I heard about a fresh outpouring of the Holy Spirit at a church near the airport in Toronto, and I felt compelled to visit and investigate this phenomena for myself. For several years, I attended both the Catholic Church and Toronto Airport Christian Fellowship. It was not an easy decision, but finally I made the Airport Church, now called Catch The Fire Toronto, my home, and I remain to this day.

This devotional was birthed some 15 years ago at a Charismatic Prayer Group when one of the leaders said prophetically to me, "Michael, God wants you to write a book". I had never considered writing a book and was astonished by this prophecy, so I took no action. But a few months later, I awoke early one cold winter's morning with an absolute conviction that God did indeed want me to write a book. In my spirit, I knew exactly what He wanted me to write. I jumped out of bed and wrote down the List of Contents for this book as if I was taking dictation from the Lord. I completed the first outline in five days, over the Christmas holidays. As someone who had never written anything longer than a business report in the past, I knew that God was clearly involved.

Since I didn't know anything about publishing, the manuscript sat on the shelf for several years. Later, I submitted it to a contest for Christian writers and received positive feedback from the judges; but again, I put it back on the shelf. I wasn't certain that a commercial publisher would be interested in the work, nor did I want to self-publish, only to store the books in my basement and give them away to family and friends. Something was missing. Now, after many setbacks and false starts, the book is finally published as a devotional, and I am deeply honoured that Catch The Fire Books has agreed to partner with me in this endeavor. They were possibly more excited than I was. Who knew!

As you read and meditate on each daily message, my prayer for you is based on Aaron's blessing (Numbers 6:24-26).

May God bless you and keep you. May He let His face shine upon you. And be gracious to you. May He uncover His face to you, And bring you even closer into His heart. May you rise up—on eagles' wings.

A Cry for Help

In my distress I called to the LORD; I cried to my God for help. From his
temple he heard my voice; my cry came before him, into his ears.

PSALM 18:6

He said: "In my distress I called to the LORD, and he answered me. From
deep in the realm of the dead I called for help, and you listened to my cry."

JONAH 2:2

We've all cried out to God at sometime, haven't we? I can
remember a time when I cried out to Him in pure despera-
tion; it was more than forty years ago, just five days after the
birth of our first child, Stephen. I came to visit my wife Marion
and our new born son in the hospital, expecting to take them
home, but when I got to their room I could see that something
was dreadfully wrong. Marion described how, when the nurse
brought Stephen to her for feeding she immediately saw that
he was in distress; and upon investigation discovered that
his lower body was black. He was rushed into the emergency
department where the doctors determined that he had a tear
in his intestine and the resulting infection was leaking into his
bloodstream. They told us that he urgently needed surgery but
they wanted to transfer him to a teaching hospital in London,
Ontario, where they had specialized facilities for operating on
newborn infants. London was about one hour's drive away.

Marion remained in hospital overnight, and since I was not allowed to travel in the ambulance, I followed after by car. Fortunately we had relatives in London and they were wonderfully supportive of us during this ordeal. It was while I was driving to London that, through my tears, I cried out to God. I'm not sure exactly what I said, but I'm pretty sure my cry went something like this; "Help God help! Please save our baby! Don't take him from us. It's not fair to take him now. Help God! Help!" And then I distinctly remember adding "Lord, if you do save him, I will serve you for the rest of my life."

Now I know you are not supposed to bargain with God like this, but desperate times call for desperate measures, don't they? And God did save Stephen. He survived the surgery and recovered quickly; we brought him home in three weeks. Not only that but he grew up to be strong and healthy. He played hockey and baseball as a child, switching to lacrosse as a teen and later played field lacrosse for the University of Western Ontario. At University he started weight training and later became a fitness coach. Today he is married with three beautiful children.

So God did hear my cry and he did save Stephen. And I believe that He honoured the second part of my prayer as well, by calling me into His service. I'm still in His service today. Would this have happened anyway? I don't know, but I do hope to find out when we meet face to face.

Are you desperate for help today? Then why not cry out to Him? What do you have to lose? Even if you have doubts or questions, you can still cry out for answers. As I look around the world today I still have questions. Why is the world in such a mess? Why is there so much poverty, famine, war, sickness and evil? I don't have all the answers to these questions but I do know from practical experience that God does answer prayer. The first step in your journey of discovery and healing is to share your needs with Him.

Here's a prayer to guide you:

Help me God, help me! You know my situation (name it) *and I am now turning to you for help. I've tried other solutions, but they are not working well. You are the God of all creation, You can do miracles, You can do this …*

God help me to believe in you more and to trust you with this situation. Give me wisdom to cooperate with your solution, And not to insist on doing things my way. Show me what to do and what not to do, And how to step back, let go, and trust you.

Finally God, I really do want to get to know you better, And to establish a closer relationship with you. As I read this devotional give me more insight into yourself, Come teach me your ways.

Further Meditation

Can you think of a time when God answered your prayer? Write your answer below:

_____

_____

_____

_____

_____

_____

_____

_____

_____

_____

What can you learn from this experience?

_____

_____

_____

_____

_____

_____

_____

_____

_____

_____

Meeting Jesus

But you, He said, who do you say I am? Then Simon Peter spoke up. You are
the Christ, he said, the Son of the living God.

MATTHEW 16:15

The woman said to Him, "I know that the Messiah (called Christ) is com-
ing". When He comes, He will tell us all things. Then Jesus declared, "I, the
one speaking to you—I am he."

JOHN 4:25-26

I find that the stories of Jesus' life in the Bible are so inspiring,
so wonderful, so encouraging. They reveal how He:

- » Was born in a humble stable, and grew to manhood
  without fuss or fanfare.
- » Preached conversion from sin, healed the sick and
  cast out demons.
- » Befriended the poor and disenfranchised of his time.
- » Died on a cross for the sins of the world.
- » Rose from the dead after three days and ascended
  into Heaven.
- » Showed us by His life, how to live and how to
  renounce selfishness and sin.
- » Gave us the great commandment: to love God and
  to love others.

» Taught us about His Father's love for us.
» Sent us His Holy Spirit to be with us for all eternity.

Once I understood that the Jesus described in these stories is still alive in Heaven today, and that He wants a relationship with me, then I had to respond somehow. And as I responded by spending more time in prayer He seemed to draw me in, deeper and deeper. As I read the Bible I began to have a personal relationship with Jesus as a man and a friend, rather than just knowing *about* Him as a historical figure. I was able to see myself in the various stories and they became more real to me. The Bible became a living book, not just a historical story.

I came to realize that when Jesus, who is fully God, became man 2000 years ago, He left his claim to divinity in Heaven and walked the earth just as you and I do, fully human. In a similar way Prince Harry, the current Prince of Wales, did not claim any royal privilege when he was serving his country in the armed forces; instead he put on army uniform and was treated by his peers like any other soldier. So it was with Jesus, when He was living on Earth. He did not rely on his Divine powers; He simply did what He heard His Father say and used the power of the Holy Spirit to guide His every step.

As a man, Jesus knew pain, hunger, and thirst. He also experienced rejection and betrayal and every human emotion including sadness, joy and even anger. When He awoke in the morning He did not know what the day would bring, He just allowed it to unfold, always listening in the Spirit to what His Father wanted Him to do. And today He wants to continue His mission on earth, but through each one of us. We have become His hands and His feet. He lives in us and through us, as the following scripture indicates.

> Therefore go and make disciples of all nations, baptizing them in the name of the Father and of the Son and of the Holy Spirit, and teaching them to obey everything I have commanded you. And surely I am with you always, to the very end of the age.
>
> MATTHEW 28:19-20

This may feel like a daunting task; let's ask for His help:

Jesus help me to know you better. To really believe that you are the Saviour of the world, And my personal Saviour.

I am sorry that I have not always acted in ways that are pleasing to you; forgive me. I want to start again and live according to your will.

Jesus you came to save all peoples from sin and sickness, and to save me from my own ignorance of you.

Help me to love you, as you love me, and to love others, as you love them. Allow me to be a source of your love and light to this troubled world.

But mostly Jesus, enable me to have a personal, relationship with you. To know you as my Lord and Saviour, But also as my brother and friend. A friend who loves and supports me—despite my failures.

I believe that if I have this personal relationship with you, my cares and worries will be so much lighter, because this is what you have promised in scripture.

Come, Lord Jesus, fill me with your love, your Spirit. Jesus, I trust you to answer this prayer as I place my trust in you.

Further Meditation

Do you know Jesus personally, or do you just know about him?

_____

_____

_____

_____

_____

_____

Would you like to know him better, as a friend? Then ask Him, in your own words.

_____

_____

_____

_____

_____

_____

Welcoming the Holy Spirit

All this I have spoken while still with you. But the Advocate, the Holy
Spirit, *whom the Father will send in my name, will teach you all things
and will remind you of everything I have said to you.*

JOHN 14:25-26

And if the Spirit *of him who raised Jesus from the dead is living in you, he
who raised Christ from the dead will also give life to your mortal bodies
because of his* Spirit *who lives in you.*

ROMANS 8:11

In the original Hebrew text, the word commonly translated as
Spirit is *ruach*, which means breath or wind. The Greek word
that we interpret as Spirit is *pneuma* which means current of
air, wind or breath. So the Holy Spirit can be thought of as
the breath of God, the very life-force of God. We see from the
scriptures that God breathed His life into creation: *And the
LORD God formed man of the dust of the ground, and breathed into
his nostrils the breath of life; and man became a living soul (Genesis
1:1),* and He breathes His Spirit into us again when we receive
Him into our lives (Romans 8:11).

Jesus told us much about the Holy Spirit and the role of the
Spirit today. He said the Holy Spirit will:

» Be our advocate (supporter, helper, and backer). John 14:25
» Teach us all things. John 14:26

» Remind us of everything Christ said. John 14:26

» Help us bear witness of Christ. John 15:26

» Reveal the righteousness of Christ. John 16:10

» Guide us in all truth. John 16:13

» Reveal the future to believers. John 16:13

» Be our counselor. John 16:16

» Convict unbelievers of their sin. John 16:16

» Empower believers with spiritual power. Acts 1:8

» Empower believers to be powerful witnesses for Christ. Matthew 28:20

In his devotional book *Unshakable Faith*[1] Pastor Rick Joyner writes that The Holy Spirit is the agent of God who does the work. He is ever moving, working and bringing forth the purposes of God. It is crucial for every Christian to know the Holy Spirit and learn how to follow Him in all things.

Scripture also teaches us that The Holy Spirit brings us the gifts of wisdom, understanding, counsel, power, and deep reverence for God (Isaiah 11:2). These gifts are confirmed and extended in 1 Corinthians 12-13 as gifts of wisdom, knowledge, expectant faith, healing, miraculous powers, prophecy, discernment, speaking in tongues and the interpretation of tongues. This latter set of gifts, sometimes called the charismatic gifts, was bestowed by the Holy Spirit to the apostles at Pentecost and continues to be given to us today.

I will reveal more about this Pentecost experience and what it has meant to me in Day 15, but for now let's welcome the

---

[1]   Rick Joyner, Unshakable Faith, Destiny Image, 2000, page 19.

Holy Spirit and invite Him to be our guide, teacher and provider of every gift that we need.

Let's pray:

Holy Spirit I welcome you. Come open my mind and my heart, guide me and teach me in your ways, and lead me into deeper revelation of you...

Help me not to dwell on my own shortcomings, or focus on the evil I see around me, but experience your wisdom and love.

Give me the spiritual gifts I need, right now, to follow you. Fill me with your wisdom, understanding, counsel, and love of the Lord my God.

Come Holy Spirit, fill me with your love, your presence. Fill me with your power, and bring me into a personal relationship with you.

Come Holy Spirit, come!

Further Meditation

Do you know the Holy Spirit as your personal guide and helper?

_____

_____

_____

_____

_____

_____

_____

_____

_____

_____

Which of His special gifts would you ask for? Why?

_____

_____

_____

_____

_____

_____

_____

_____

_____

_____

_____

Encountering the Father

Jesus replied, "Anyone who loves me will obey my teaching. My Father will love them, and we will come to them and make our home with them.

JOHN 14:23

The Spirit you received does not make you slaves, so that you live in fear again; rather, the Spirit you received brought about your adoption to sonship. And by him we cry, "Abba, Father."

ROMANS 8:15

Have you ever struggled with the idea of God as your father? I certainly have. As a child I pictured The Father as someone to be feared rather than loved. I imagined Him as an ancient person with a white beard appearing with thunder and lightning; rather like Charlton Heston in the movie "The Ten Commandments". So in my ignorance, I concluded that The Father was not someone I wanted to spend much time with, or approach too closely! Yet Jesus taught us to call our heavenly Father, *Abba*. Many have suggested that in today's language this could be rendered Daddy. If you go to Israel today you can still hear young children calling their fathers, *Abba*.

In Luke chapter 15 verses 11-32 (the parable of the Prodigal Son), we read the story of the father and his rebellious son: how the son goes to his dad and asks for his inheritance. When he receives this fortune he goes off and squanders it by loose living. Yet his father loves him enough to let him leave and learn some of life's hard lessons for himself. When the son finally comes to his senses and returns home, his father greets him with great joy, forgives him even before he asks, and throws a great party for him. Don't we all wish for this kind of dad? One that is loving and compassionate; quick to forgive when we make mistakes.

Jesus came to earth in order to reveal His Father to us and He did so in the parable above. God our heavenly Father is a loving father and He is waiting for you and for me to come home. He is waiting to forgive us, to put His best robe around our shoulders and a ring on our finger. He is waiting to welcome us into His house for a heavenly feast that will last for all eternity.

A few years ago, I had an amazing encounter with The Father. Similar to a dream, or a vision, I experienced through my spirit that I was in the ballroom of a grand palace, rather like the Palace of Versailles in Paris. It was very ornate with rich tapestries on the walls, gold inlaid furniture, sparkling chandeliers and thick, lush carpets covering marble floors. And there was I, a small child in short pants. God The Father came in, smiled at me, and then picked me up by my hands and started whirling me around in a circular motion, like an airplane. Eventually we both became dizzy and collapsed to the ground laughing and giggling, and then He started to tickle me. This is how I picture The Father now, a total contrast to the stern authority figure I pictured as a child.

I suspect that many of us still have problems believing that God the Father is indeed a loving God. The problem may stem from the teachings you heard as a child or because of painful childhood experiences with your own biological father, or other authority figures. Maybe these words that Jesus spoke about His Father will help you reframe your understanding as they did for me.

I am the Way, the Truth and the Life.

No one can come to the Father except through me.

If you know me, you know my Father too.

From this moment you know him and have seen him.

JOHN 14:7

You must believe me when I say

That I am in the Father and the Father is in me.

JOHN 14:10

The Father and I are one.

JOHN 10:30

Let's pray:

Heavenly Father, may I call you Abba? I want to but Father I feel so unworthy.

Help me Father to know you as my loving Father, who loves me unconditionally, and wants only good things for me.

Help me to love you as Jesus loves you.

Father, forgive me, for I have sinned in what I have done, and in what I have failed to do. I am sorry, and want to change and do better.

I want to come home to you, Abba to be with you, now and forever.

I want to develop a closer relationship with you. Show me how, Abba, show me how.

Further Meditation

Can you picture Father God as your Abba, your Daddy?

_____

_____

_____

_____

_____

_____

_____

What would you say to Him?

_____

_____

_____

_____

_____

_____

_____

Acknowledging the Three-in-One God

I believe in one God,

The Father, the Almighty. Maker of heaven and earth.

I believe in the Lord Jesus Christ, the only Son of God.

For us men and for our salvation he came down from heaven.

For our sake he was crucified, died and was buried.

On the third day he rose again, in fulfillment of the scriptures.

I believe in the Holy Spirit,

The Lord, the giver of life.

Who proceeds from the Father and the Son.

With the Father and Son He is worshipped and glorified.

These words, taken from the Nicene Creed, were composed during the very early days of the Church in AD 325. They remain the foundation of Christian faith to this day. Non Christians and even some Christians may find these words baffling or even absurd. What do they mean for me, they wonder? What impact do they have on my life?

For me they mean that we worship one God. But this God exists as a complexity of three persons. Father, Son and Holy Spirit, equal in nature; but separate in purpose; they are coequal and coeternal—one God yet three individual expressions (persons) of that God. As I pondered this mystery over the years, I have found the following images helpful (though

I am not sure that any human description can fully penetrate this mystery of the three-in-one-God; which we also call The Trinity):

First, suppose you went to the store and bought a family sized tub of Neapolitan ice-cream; made up of three flavours, vanilla, strawberry and chocolate. And suppose the flavours were combined together in one big swirl, so that when you scooped the ice-cream out of the tub you would find all three flavours in the same scoop. Would you not have a three-in-one serving of ice-cream; three flavours, one ice-cream?

The second image is that of a high mountain peak covered in snow and ice. This mountain has three prominent faces, and if we were able to hire a helicopter and fly around the summit we would see three very different faces. The first a sheer drop into a glacier below, the second a more gradual rocky slope into an alpine meadow, and the third a craggy ridge leading to a lower summit. You would have experienced one mountain yet three very different aspects or faces.

I learned this third image from healing evangelist Benny Hinn at a conference I recently attended. He made the point that we humans are made in the image and likeness of God. *"So God created mankind in his own image, in the image of God he created them; male and female he created them" (Genesis 1:27).* Then he went on to say that scripture also states that we too have three essential elements; body, soul and spirit. *"May God himself, the God of peace, sanctify you through and through. May your whole **spirit, soul and body** be kept blameless at the coming of our*

Lord Jesus Christ" (*1 Thessalonians 5:23*).[2] So we too have a Three-in-One nature (spirit, soul and body); not equal to God's, but reflective of Him.

Finally I had an experience of what The Trinity might be like. One night as I was in prayer I saw, with my spirit, a shaft of white light, and I had the sense that this was the presence of God. As I approached I could see that the light was actually three individual columns of light. The columns appeared to be like three persons standing in a circle holding hands, just enjoying each other's company. In my spirit I sensed that they were Father, Son and Holy Spirit. As I approached even closer they parted and I was invited to enter into their circle. As I did so I felt an immense sense of peace and love; something words can hardly describe. How long I was in this state I do not know. When I "came to" I was at perfect peace and within my heart at least, the mystery of The Trinity had been resolved.

Let's pray:

O God of mystery, Father, Son and Holy Spirit. I thank you for revealing yourself in scripture, in nature and in the everyday experiences of life.

---

2   My understanding is that the soul comprises our mind, will and emotions— that is our personality. and the spirit is that place where we connect with God, see visions and communicate with Him. Our spirit is primary and is meant to provide leadership to the soul, which in turn leads the body. We *are* spirit, *have* a soul and live *in* a body.

I cannot begin to say that I understand all that you are or all you have said and done. But I want to grow in faith and understanding of You.

Prepare a space in my heart that nurtures further knowledge of you. I open myself to you, right now and I ask you to teach me more.

More about the Father, my creator, more about Jesus, my saviour, more about the Holy Spirit, my teacher and comforter.

Lord God, I'm seeking more revelation of you, show me more.

Further Meditation

How do you relate to the 3-in-1 God?

_____

_____

_____

_____

_____

_____

_____

_____

_____

_____

_____

_____

_____

DAY 6

Accepting Salvation

For God so loved the world that He gave His one and only son, that whoever believes in Him shall not perish but may have eternal life.

JOHN 3:16

Christ died for us while we were still sinners; this proves how much God loves us.

ROMANS 5:8

What is salvation? In the Old Testament the word for salvation is Yeshuah, which means to save, deliver, heal and prosper; this was also the name given by the angel Gabriel to Mary when he told her she was to be the mother of the Messiah.[3] In the New Testament the Greek word for salvation is *sozo*, which also translates to save, heal and deliver. I understand the concept of salvation as saving us from our sins and from the punishment of those sins, which is eternal death; it also includes healing us from all physical, emotional and spiritual sicknesses, quite literally delivering us from evil and Satan's hold over us. Both the Old and New Testament are filled with stories about how God saved, healed and delivered His people, but you may wonder if He is still doing this today? You bet He is! Let me give you an example.

---

3   Matthew 1:21

A few years ago I was asked by a prison chaplain to work with a man who seemed severely depressed and disoriented—I'll call him Tony although that is not his real name. He mostly sat by himself with his head bowed low, rarely speaking, yet always clutching a small red pocket Bible. Over a series of weekly meetings he eventually told me his story. He was raised in a good Christian home and had been with the Canadian Armed Forces engaged in the peacekeeping effort in Bosnia. There he had witnessed some of the atrocities of war, including the death of his best friend, who was blown up by a landmine and died in his arms.

When he returned to his family in Canada he was not the same man they knew, and he ultimately tried to commit suicide. He told me how he took a large kitchen knife and slit open his throat, and as he did this he looked up to heaven and cried out "God you can't save me this time". When he awoke he was in hospital and the doctor who had just completed surgery asked him what drugs he was taking. Tony replied, "I'm not taking any drugs". The doctor explained that Tony had almost completely severed the artery in his neck and lost so much blood that they did not think they could save him. Then the impossible happened: the blood in his neck clotted by itself and they were able to repair the wound. The doctor explained that what had occurred wasn't medically possible, he had never seen or heard of it happening before. Tony then remembered how he had cried out, "God you can't save me." With an instant change of heart, he repented for his actions, re-committed his life to Jesus and accepted salvation.

It was only when Tony was in prison that he was diagnosed

with Post Traumatic Stress Disorder and eventually moved
to a psychiatric hospital where he received the treatment he
needed. So, yes, even in the midst of this very tragic story, you
can see that God is still in the saving business.

Even if you haven't experienced such an extreme miracle in
your own life, there have probably been countless times when
God has blessed you without you being aware of it. God always
knows what you need even if the complete solution hasn't been
revealed to you yet. Jesus came to show us how much God
loves us. By his life, death and resurrection, he showed us this
love. Today, He wants every one of us to believe in Him, and
to accept Him as our Lord and Saviour.

Here is a very simple prayer to commit or to re-commit your
life to Jesus and accept salvation:

*Lord Jesus, I believe that you are the Son of God, that you came down
from Heaven fully human and lived among us. That you died on the
cross for me, and on the third day you rose again*

*Jesus, I admit that I am a sinner and have gone my own way. I'm sorry
for my sins, and I ask for your forgiveness. I am ready to return to you.*

*I ask you, Lord Jesus, to come into my heart, and to be the Lord of my
life. I accept you as my Lord and Savior. I give my life to you. Amen.*

If you prayed this prayer, God will hear and answer you—
that's guaranteed. But in order to grow spiritually, you will
need to take some actions of your own. If you are not presently

a member of a church, I urge you to make every effort to find a community of Christians to Join. Maybe you know a Christian in your family, or work, who will help you find a church that is right for you.

I also recommend the website, bornofthespirit.today. This site contains a wealth of information regarding salvation and how you can deepen your relationship with God.

Further Meditation

Whether you prayed this prayer for the first time, or were recommitting your life to Jesus, ask the Lord about your next step in growing closer to Him?

_____

_____

_____

_____

_____

_____

_____

_____

_____

_____

_____

_____

_____

Learning to Pray

And when you pray, do not keep on babbling like pagans, for they think they
will be heard because of their many words. Do not be like them, for your
Father knows what you need before you ask him.

This, then, is how you should pray:
Our Father in heaven, hallowed be your name,
Your kingdom come, your will be done, on earth as it is in heaven.
Give us today our daily bread.
And forgive us our debts, as we also have forgiven our debtors.
And lead us not into temptation, but deliver us from the evil one.

MATTHEW 6:7-13

Growing up, I used mostly formal prayers that I read out of a
prayer book. Later I was introduced to conversational prayers,
the sort I am using in this book. Later still, I learned how to
listen to God as He was speaking to me and was able to have
a two-way conversation with Him. I think that's what prayer
is all about, having a conversation with God.

One of the books on prayer that had a profound influence
on me is called *Prayers of Life* by Michel Quoist.[4] Michel died in
1997 but his books are still being published and are available
in bookstores and online. *Prayers of Life* is a collection of prayers

---

4   Michel Quoist, Prayers of Life, Gill and MacMillan, Translation Sheed &
     Ward Inc, 1963.

and meditations that deal with some of the very gritty and difficult aspects of life, such as hunger, poverty, death, doubt, addiction and sin. Yet even within these issues God's presence is found. This book taught me that I can and should pray about all the messy parts of my life. What's the use of trying to hide all this stuff from God? After all He already knows all about it. I realized that prayer is not about being holy, or putting on a front before Him, it's about coming before Him as I am and being real. I can bring all of my problems and even my sin to Him, talk about them, and ask what God thinks and wants me to do about them. What's His plan, His solution?

Jesus himself teaches us how to pray in Matthew chapter 6. Let's examine the structure of what we call The Lord's Prayer.

» Notice that in Matthew, before Jesus reveals this prayer, He asks us not to babble and use a lot of complicated words. In other words, we are to keep it short, simple and from the heart.

» Then He asks us to acknowledge Him as our Father, to praise Him and to enter into His presence, as best we can.

» Next we place His will above our will. After all, He knows us intimately and wants only the very best for us. When we follow our own will, often we chase after things that are not essential or even good for us.

» Then, as we ask for our needs, we do this from a heavenly perspective and try to be aware of what He wants for us. What is His plan for us?

» As we ask forgiveness for our sins, we first forgive others for what they have done against us.

» Finally we ask for God's protection. This includes protection from all accidents, sickness and harm; both in the physical and spiritual realm.

Here is a prayer, based on the Lord's Prayer:

Abba, Father, teach me to pray.

I praise you for just being yourself, for being the Lord and Creator of all, and being my Lord, my God and my eternal Father.

I praise you and thank you for all you have done, and are doing, in my life and I come seeking your heart for me.

Abba, I come to you asking forgiveness for all my offenses and I forgive all those who have offended me. (Pause and bring to mind those you need to forgive).

Now Abba I bring before you some of the messy parts of my life, My fears, my doubts, my sin ... (name them), *and ask for your help.*

I place myself in your care and I ask only for those things that you desire for me. Guide me to know and to submit to your will.

I ask you to protect me, my family and friends From all evil, and from all accidents, sickness and harm.

I praise you Father, Son and Holy Spirit, and give you all honor and glory, now and forever, Amen.

Further Meditation

How often do you think we should pray?

_____

_____

_____

_____

_____

_____

_____

_____

How often do you pray?

_____

_____

_____

_____

_____

_____

_____

_____

On the following pages you will find two more prayers that you may wish to pray as part of your daily devotion…

Daily Offering Prayer

Jesus, I love you and praise your holy name. I thank you for all that you have done for me and I return to you all that I am.

I give you my mind that it may become like the mind of Christ. I give you my heart that it may always love you. I give you my spirit that I will dwell in your presence forever.

I give you my eyes that I may see as you see, my ears that I may hear when you speak to me, my lips that I may always proclaim your words, and my hands and feet that I may work in your perfect will.

Jesus, I give you every thought, word and deed of my life. I place my family and all my possessions in your care.

And I offer all for you honor and glory. Amen.

Daily Prayer for Guidance

Lord God, help me to live your will for my life today. To love you as my Father, my Savior and my sanctifier.

To actively seek your will for me at all times, to listen and be open to your voice and to be faithful in serving you in my family, my friends and my community.

Lord, help me to love my neighbor, to never intentionally hurt anyone, to keep my marriage vows, a and to honor and love my children.

Finally Lord, help me to love myself; to take care of myself physically, emotionally and spiritually. To control my thoughts, my emotions and my motivation, and to live life to the fullest with joy and hope.

Grant me this so that we can dwell together this day and forever. I ask this prayer in Jesus name, Amen.

Glorifying the Name of Jesus

*She will give birth to a son and you are to give him the **name Jesus**, because he will save his people from their sins.*

MATTHEW 1:21

*And in that day you will ask Me nothing. Most assuredly, I say to you, whatever you ask the Father **in My name** He will give you.*

JOHN 16:23

I think we all understand the significance of brand names like Apple, Ford, Pepsi, and so on. For the most part we are confident that "brand name" products will perform well and that the manufacturer will stand behind any warranty that is given. But have you ever thought that this same confidence and warranty might apply to God's name—in fact, infinitely more so?

In Jewish tradition, a person's name signifies something important about his or her character or trade. This is why it is so significant that the angel of the Lord told Joseph to name the child Jesus. In Hebrew, the name Jesus (Yeshua) means "Yahweh saves", in other words, "God saves". And Christ means "the anointed one of God". So the name Jesus Christ means "the anointed One of God who brings salvation."

Part of Jesus' mission is to heal, save and deliver His people from all physical, emotional and spiritual sickness. We have God's promise and warranty on that!

The Apostle Paul had great reverence for the name of Jesus when he wrote:

*"But God raised Him high and gave the **name that is above every name**, that at the name of Jesus all beings in heaven, on the earth and in the underworld should bend the knee and shall bow down and every tongue confess that Jesus Christ is Lord, to the Glory of God the Father."*

PHILIPPIANS 2:8

The early Christians experienced the authority and awesome power of Jesus' name as they went about healing the sick, and casting out demons in His name.

*These are the signs that will follow those who believe: **in my name** they will cast out devils...they will lay their hands on the sick and they will recover.*

MARK 16:17-18 NKJV

*The seventy-two came back rejoicing. Lord, they said, even the devils submit to us when **we use your name**.*

LUKE 10:17

*... Peter said (to the cripple) "In the **name of Jesus Christ** the Nazarene, walk!"*

ACTS 3:6

*Is anyone among you sick? Let them call the elders of the church to pray over them and anoint them with oil in the **name of the Lord**. And the prayer offered in faith will make the sick person well; the Lord will raise them up. If they have sinned, they will be forgiven.*

JAMES 5:14-15

Later in this book we will explore, in some depth, the authority and healing power we have in the name of Jesus. For now let's praise Him and give glory to His holy name with this prayer below. We give Him glory, not because He needs it, but because we need it. We need to remind ourselves of whom He is and what He has done for us. We are not adding to God's glory by praising Him, nothing can add to His glory. Instead as we praise Him we are acknowledging His presence and reality in our lives and our need for Him.

I invite you to pray this prayer out loud:

Father God, I praise the mighty name of your Son, Jesus. Holy, holy, holy is His name.

Jesus, you are the Lord of Lords, and the King of Kings, glory be your name.

Jesus you are the alpha and the omega, the beginning and the end, glory be your name.

Jesus, Lamb of God glory be your name.

Jesus, you are my rock and my salvation, glory be your name.

Jesus, you are the way, the truth and the light of the world, glory be your name.

Jesus, you are my Good Shepherd, glory be your name.

Jesus, you are my healer, my friend, my brother, glory be your name.

Jesus, you are my Lord and my God, glory be your name.

All honor and glory are yours, O Jesus, forever and ever. Amen.

Further Meditation

What else in your life can you glorify Jesus for?

_____

_____

_____

_____

_____

_____

_____

_____

_____

_____

_____

_____

_____

_____

_____

_____

_____

Jesus, the Good Shepherd

I myself will tend my sheep and have them lie down, declares the Sovereign LORD. I will search for the lost and bring back the strays. I will bind up the injured and strengthen the weak ... I will shepherd the flock with justice.

EZEKIEL 34:15-16

Here is the Lord God coming with power ... He is like a shepherd feeding his flock, gathering the lambs in his arms, holding them closely into his breast and leading them to a place of rest.

ISAIAH 40:10

The LORD is my shepherd; I shall not want. He makes me to lie down in green pastures; He leads me beside the still waters. He restores my soul; He leads me in the paths of righteousness For His name's sake.

Yea, though I walk through the valley of the shadow of death, I will fear no evil; for You are with me; Your rod and Your staff, they comfort me.

You prepare a table before me in the presence of my enemies; You anoint my head with oil; My cup runs over. Surely goodness and mercy shall follow me all the days of my life; and I will dwell in the house of the LORD Forever.

PSALM 23:1-6

Growing up in England I was accustomed to seeing lots of

sheep in the fields. I remember going to country fairs and watching in fascination as sheep dogs, under the direction of a shepherd, guided a flock of sheep around an obstacle course and into a sheep-pen. It wasn't until later that I understood the significance of shepherds in biblical times.

In those days the country of Israel was unfenced, so in the early morning the shepherd would separate his flock from the others in the sheepfold, and lead them out to pasture. His flock would recognize his voice and follow only him. During the day he would watch over them, making sure that none wandered away. He would also have to lead them to fresh water, either a quiet stream or a well with drinking troughs. Did you know that sheep will not drink from turbulent water; they only drink from still water? The shepherd would also tend to all their injuries and sicknesses, so he was also their vet. In the evening he would lead them back to the sheepfold and it was his responsibility to guard them from wild animals and thieves through the night. Sometimes he would lie down to sleep across the entrance, to ensure nothing entered the pen. In today's terminology this would be called a 24/7 job!

It is interesting that in the Old Testament the term shepherd was also used to describe the priests (pastors) of that time. In Ezekiel chapter 34 (above) God first delivered a stern rebuke to the leaders of that time because they were not looking after the people as they should; then He said that He Himself would shepherd His flock. So when God said that He himself would shepherd his people, this was a prophetic word concerning the role of Jesus, The Messiah.

Jesus confirmed this when he said …

I am the good shepherd, I know my own and my own know me, just as my Father knows me and I know the Father: and I lay down my life for my sheep...
I am the gate (of the sheepfold). Anyone who enters through me will be safe, he will go freely in and out, and be sure of finding pasture ...
The sheep that belong to me listen to my voice, I know them and they follow me;
I give them eternal life ... (Extracted from John 10:1-30)

When Jesus said, "I am the good shepherd", His disciples knew he was talking in the spiritual and not the physical, sense. Jesus came to take care of his people in every spiritual and physical need: protect them, lead them, feed them, heal them, and ultimately to die for them. And that is precisely what He did for them, and for you and me.

I'd like to share with you two stories of how God continues to provide for us and how He "prepares a table before us".[5] Both stories occurred at a Christian drop-in centre where I have the privilege of serving. On one recent occasion, a lady with three children came in right before Christmas to say that she had just lost her job and desperately needed gifts and groceries. Could we help? The staff asked her to make a list of things she needed and the lady listed eleven items. As the staff searched the cupboards they found only one item from the list, and then prayed for the Lord to provide the remaining items. Three hours later another lady, who had previously been helped at the drop-in centre, brought in several bags of Christmas gifts

---

5   Psalm 23:5

and groceries that she had just bought at a nearby shopping mall. As the staff unpacked these bags they found all of the items that they had been praying for. In only three hours, The Lord Jesus did indeed supply all eleven items on this family's wish list. This was no coincidence; it's the nature of God, our Good Shepherd.

The second story is even more amazing because it involves a wonder of "multiplication", similar to how Jesus fed five thousand people when they were in an isolated place and evening was approaching.[6] Again it occurred around Christmas time, but this time the drop-in centre staff was serving a meal for about 40 people. As they came to serve dessert they found that they had only one Christmas cake made in the shape of a Yule-time log, large enough to serve about eight or ten people. With a sad heart the server started to cut the cake, knowing that it would not be sufficient for everyone. After she had cut several pieces she realized that the cake was not reducing in size and so, with joyful tears streaming down her face, she continued to cut ... and cut ... and cut ... until there was enough for everyone, with some left over. Afterwards she said that she dared not stop slicing the cake, in case the miracle stopped! Wow, isn't it wonderful that Jesus, The Good Shepherd, is still taking care of His flock!

You may have faced times of scarcity and times of plenty over the years. There may have been times when a solution to a problem suddenly presented itself, but you may not have recognized it was God caring for you.

---

6   Matthew 14:13

Let this prayer below remind you that God cares for you and will meet your needs. Add to it as you wish to suit your situation.

Thank you Jesus, for you are my good shepherd. You lead me to good pasture, and provide for all my needs. You refresh me and restore my strength.

Even when I am going through difficult times, I know that you are there, looking after me and guiding my steps. Help me, Lord, to hear your voice and to respond to your call.

So Jesus, I ask you to take care of all my physical needs, my financial needs, my healthcare needs, my emotional needs and my spiritual needs.

To comfort and recharge me when I am tired or upset, and to protect me from all the attacks of my enemies, Thank you Jesus, my good shepherd. I place my life into your care, Amen.

Further Meditation

Do you have a special need to pray for? Make a list and pray in faith for Jesus to supply all your needs according to His will.

_____

_____

_____

_____

Jesus, the True Vine

You transplanted a vine from Egypt; you drove out the nations and planted it.
Return to us, God Almighty! Look down from heaven and see! Watch over
this vine, the root your right hand has planted, the son you have raised up
for yourself.

PSALM 80:8, 14-15

I am the true vine, and my Father is the vine dresser ...
Abide in Me, and I in you. As the branch cannot bear fruit of itself, unless
it abides in the vine, neither can you, unless you abide in Me. I am the vine,
you are the branches. He who abides in Me, and I in him, bears much fruit;
for without Me you can do nothing.

JOHN 15:1, 4-5 NKJV

It took me a long time to discover the richness of the Bible and how closely interconnected the New Testament and the Old Testament are. History shows us that the Bible was written by Jews and a good part of the New Testament was written for Jewish followers of Jesus. So to understand the words of Jesus, it greatly helps to approach them from a Jewish perspective. I'm fortunate to have a good friend who is a Messianic Jew; that is a Jew who believes that Jesus was and is the promised Messiah. He is steeped in the Torah, and celebrates the best of both Jewish and Christian traditions, just as the early Christians did. I tease him and say he has the best of both worlds.

In the Old Testament readings (above), the nation of Israel is referred to as a vine and also personalized as a son. So when Jesus referred to himself as the "True Vine", I believe his hearers would have understood the spiritual significance of His words. He was metaphorically saying "I am the nation of Israel, I am the Son of God" and He goes on to talk about his Father as the vine dresser, or gardener. It is He who planted the vine and also cares for it, prunes it and will ultimately harvest the fruit. In Romans 11:13-24 Paul explains that gentiles (non-Jewish people) have been grafted onto this vine and are the spiritual sons and daughters of Abraham.

Abiding (soaking) in Jesus

Of course vines need nourishing water to survive, and water imagery resounds through Christian literature as well. Jesus said "Abide in Me", but how do we do this? I think that perhaps the best way is to simply rest and allow Him to come to us. At my church we call this soaking and it's as simple as sitting or lying down peacefully, playing worship music, and letting God come to us in thoughts and images, through the presence of the Holy Spirit. Let me give you an example. One night as I was soaking at home and allowing the music to wash over me, I saw in my spirit a fountain with three basins, one below the other, each one larger than the one above it, reminding me of a Roman fountain. And as I watched I saw water cascading down from the top to the lower basins, and I had the sense that this was God's living water or grace, flowing within me. First it filled up my spirit, then my soul (in other words my mind, will and emotions) and finally it filled up my body. And at each level, this living water brought peace, transformation and healing. This image came to me for several nights in a row.

As I meditated on this "living water" I was led to the passage in which the prophet Ezekiel has a vision of the River of God flowing from the temple in the New Jerusalem.[7] The apostle John also saw this same river when he had his vision of the end-times and the New Jerusalem.[8] Jesus also spoke about these living waters, *"Whoever believes in me, as Scripture has said, rivers of living water will flow from within them"* (John 7:38-39). By this he meant the Spirit.

As for my own fountain image, imagine my surprise when some time later I discovered that St. Teresa of Avila, a 16 century Catholic mystic, had a similar vision. St. Teresa founded a number of Carmelite convents, in Spain, devoted to contemplative prayer. In her vision she saw a fountain and sensed the cascading water as God's presence flowing into her and embracing her entire being: body, soul and spirit. She was overwhelmed by the feeling of peace and love.[9] I know just how she felt.

On another occasion, a team from our church carried out this same soaking experience in a men's prison. In the prison chapel I gave a short talk on abiding in His presence, and then had the men rest quietly in chairs or lie on the floor as we played restful worship music. At the end of the service we gathered the men together and asked them to share what they had experienced. I have to admit that I was amazed to

7   Ezekiel 47:8-9, 12
8   Revelation 22:1-2
9   James W. Goll, The Lost Art of Practicing His Presence, Destiny Image, 2005, page 74.

hear their stories. One had a vision of Jesus, several others saw intense white light (the room lights had been dimmed), others felt heat and tingling throughout their bodies, others described wiping away tears of joy; and one was healed from a migraine headache. All of them knew that they had experienced the presence of God, and asked if we could repeat this soaking experience again. I can only begin to imagine the transforming effect of this experience on their lives.

I encourage you to try this soaking experience for yourself. Just find a quiet place where you can be undisturbed, leave aside anything that is worrying you, play soothing music (it doesn't necessarily matter if it's "Christian" or not), and prayerfully invite God's presence to flow into you. I believe that you too will be amazed and blessed by this experience of abiding in Him.

Let's pray:

Jesus, I believe that you are the True Vine, and that I am a (tiny) branch. Cut off from you I can do nothing!

Come now Holy Spirit and fill me with your presence, your life, your grace, your love. Help me to stay connected to you and to bear much fruit. Come abide in me. Soak me, nourish me, transform me, heal me.

I ask this in the name of Jesus.

Further Meditation

Don't say a word, just rest in His presence. Let His healing waters flow over you …

_____

_____

_____

_____

_____

_____

_____

_____

_____

_____

What do you sense God is saying to you?

_____

_____

_____

_____

_____

_____

_____

_____

_____

_____

_____

Embracing the Cross

God so loved the world that he gave his one and only Son, that whoever believes in him shall not perish but have eternal life. For God did not send his Son into the world to condemn the world, but to save the world through him.

JOHN 3:16-17

But God demonstrates his own love for us in this: While we were still sinners, Christ died for us.

ROMANS 5:8

I must admit that I had a hard time understanding, let alone embracing the cross. How could God the Father send His Son Jesus to suffer and die on the cross for our sins? What was The Father doing while Jesus was suffering this terrible death on the cross? Why couldn't He find an easier way for us to gain salvation? It didn't make much sense, and as Paul said to the early Christians in Corinth, it was a stumbling block, and an irrational one.

Jews demand signs and Greeks look for wisdom, but we preach Christ crucified: a stumbling block to Jews and foolishness to Gentiles, but to those whom God has called, both Jews and Greeks, Christ the power of God and the wisdom of God.

1 CORINTHIANS 1:22-24

As I matured as a Christian, studied scripture and listened to good preaching, the penny dropped. I came to understand that the whole point of the cross was to demonstrate just how much God loves us and how He was prepared to prove His love by suffering on the cross. And I believe that The Father and The Holy Spirit, who are so intimately connected to Jesus in the Trinity, both entered into the agony of Jesus, and suffered with Him through His ordeal. It's also interesting to note that Jesus volunteered for this mission and willingly went to the cross for us. *"Just as the Father knows me and I know the Father—and I lay down my life for the sheep. No one takes it from me, but I lay it down of my own accord. I have authority to lay it down and authority to take it up again" (John 10:15, 18).*

As I studied more in the Old Testament I learned that The Father set these events in motion from the very beginning when He called Abraham to father the nation of Israel. Blood for the Hebrew people had a very significant meaning—it was life. In Leviticus 17:11 we read "For the life of the flesh (the body, the person) is in the blood" That's why Moses sealed the Old Covenant in the blood of animals; he sprinkled half the blood on the altar and the other half on the people saying *"This is the blood of the covenant that the Lord has made with you in accordance with all these words" (Exodus 24:8).* Also when Moses led the Hebrews out of Egypt they were instructed to place the blood of lambs on the lintels and doorposts to ensure that the angels of death passed over their houses.[10]

It's also important to understand that the only way to

---

10   Exodus 12:13

forgive sin under The Old Covenant was to offer a blood sacrifice at the Tabernacle. *"Lead the goat to the bronze altar and lay your hand on its head, and have it killed. The priest will dip a finger in the blood, smear some of it on each of the four corners of the altar, and pour out the rest at the foot of the altar" (Leviticus 4:29).*

Paul summed all of this up neatly when he wrote *"In fact, the law requires that nearly everything be cleansed with blood, and without the shedding of blood there is no forgiveness" (Hebrews 9:22).* This was a God-designed exchange. The life and blood of an animal was exchanged for the spiritual life of a human. A life of sin is exchanged for a new life of forgiveness and freedom. All of this was of course a prophetic foreshadowing of Jesus, the perfect Lamb of God,[11] dying on the cross for our sins. Jesus was fully aware of all this when, at the last supper He took a cup, blessed it and said *"This is My blood, the blood of the new covenant, which will be poured for many for the forgiveness of sin" (Matthew 26:28).*

The cross is the bridge between the Old Covenant of Moses and the New Covenant of Jesus. And because the blood of Jesus was shed on the altar of the cross, our sin debt has been paid in full. How is this possible? Well suppose you have a mortgage on your home and I go to your bank and pay off your entire mortgage; how much do you owe the bank? Nothing!! That's what Jesus did for us; He paid off our sin debt in full with his own blood.

And this is only half of the Easter story. Jesus rose from the dead on the third day and in so doing He overcame death

---

11 John 1:36

for all time. And because he overcame death, we too will overcome death and live with Him for all eternity. And if that wasn't enough, The Father sent us The Holy Spirit at Pentecost to be our guide and helper in our journey along the way. He adopted us as spiritual sons and daughters so that we can claim our eternal inheritance in Him. This is the Good News of the Gospel, and the reason we can embrace the cross of Jesus.

Let's pray.

Jesus my Saviour, I thank for everything you have done for me, but especially for your dying for me on the cross.

I acknowledge that you died for my sins and that by your sacrifice I am set free: Forgiven. Saved. Healed. Redeemed.

I resolve to dedicate my life to you and I trust that you will walk beside me every step of the way.

But I can't do this alone, so I ask you Jesus to send your Holy Spirit afresh to me. To guide and instruct me and to help me embrace the cross for Jesus' sake

Thank you Father, Son and Holy Spirit for your unconditional and unlimited love. Amen.

Further Meditation

Add your own words of love and thankfulness for the cross and your salvation.

_____

_____

_____

_____

_____

_____

_____

_____

_____

_____

_____

_____

_____

_____

_____

_____

_____

_____

_____

_____

_____

_____

_____

_____

Surviving Life's Storms

As they sailed, he fell asleep. A squall came down on the lake, so that the boat was being swamped, and they were in great danger. The disciples went and woke him, saying, "Master, Master, we're going to drown!" He got up and rebuked the wind and the raging waters; the storm subsided, and all was calm.

LUKE 8:23-24

Then Peter got out of the boat and started walking towards Jesus across the water, but as soon as he felt the force of the wind he took fright and began to sink. "Lord, save me", he cried. Jesus put out His hand at once and held him. "Man of little faith", he said, "Why did you doubt"?

MATTHEW 14:29-33

Are these just nice stories, or do they apply to you and me? What can we learn from Peter's fear—and from Jesus' response? You might want to take a few moments to read the complete passage from the 14th chapter of Matthew, verses 22 to 33, and consider these questions for yourself.

I am struck by Peter's faith in getting out of the boat. I am reassured when I see his humanity as he allows fear to get the better of him and he starts to sink. Jesus' words about having little faith may seem harsh at first; but when you think about it, Jesus only said it after He reached out his hand and saved Peter. I often wonder how I would have acted in this storm.

Would I have climbed out of the boat? How far would I have walked across the water before sinking into my fears?

It is interesting that God did not prevent Peter's storm from occurring. He did not remove his fear of drowning. Rather He used all of these elements for His own purposes. I'm sure that this divine appointment changed Peter's life forever. God was in total control of the situation, even though this was not always apparent to Peter during the event.

I can relate with Peter because I think our personalities are very much alike. Before he knew Jesus, Peter was an entrepreneur running his own fishing business. He was somewhat brash and impetuous, sometimes speaking out before he had thought things through. He also went from spiritual highs to lows in quick succession. For instance, he went from witnessing Jesus' glory at the Transfiguration (Matthew 17) to denying him a short time later (Matthew 26).

For most of my business career I did not give much of the credit for my success to God, assuming that it was the result of my own skills and abilities. I prided myself on making snap decisions and was not very good at listening to others. I was aware of some of my negative personality traits but absolved myself by thinking, "God doesn't make junk, so there is nothing wrong with me!" I slid from spiritual highs to lows in quick succession. At one point I stopped going to church conferences because I knew that I would come away totally full of the Holy Spirit, only to come crashing down to earth a few days later if something went wrong in my life.

So what changed things for me? I think it was when I experienced a major career change, totally against my will. At the time I was a Vice President and General Manager, running a business unit for a major Canadian company. One day my boss came down from head-office and said "Michael, I have a new job for you; the Board has decided to get out of the business and I want you to sell off your entire operation." I was devastated but had no choice than to go along and follow his directive. I sold off the business, took the fat bonus payment and started looking for a new job.

After that experience, I had had enough of corporate life and decided to open my own Management Consulting Business. Initially, it was hard because I had to build up my own client base through networking and telephone cold calling. I quickly discovered that being self-employed actually involves being unemployed about half of the time. But I was working for myself and had more time at home with the family.

As I look back on this time, I see that God was behind this drastic change in my life and it was one of the best things that ever happened to me. I became more aware of my need for God's help every day and I would pray before making sales calls or starting new work assignments. It was around this time that I joined a Charismatic prayer group, which led to my Baptism in the Spirit which I will describe in Day 15. Later I became active in the healing ministry and experienced healing miracles, some of which I share in this book.

So now, when I am facing challenging situations I try to see my difficulties as a part of Peter's storm; the mountains of rough waves, the roar of strong winds, claps of thunder and flashes of lightning. Then I get out of my boat and set off, across the water, towards Jesus…

God does not send storms to torment us. Frequently we invite these storms into our life by our own attitudes and behaviour. As you pray this prayer let it remind you that the storms in your life are not meant to sink you. Instead they are opportunities for you to draw closer to God; and to learn how to trust Him more.

Let's pray:

Lord Jesus, I thank you for all that you have done for me, I commit myself to you today.

Sometimes Lord it is hard to hear you above all the noise and confusion in my Life. Lord, help me to hear you calling my name. Give me the strength and courage to say yes to you.

Lord, I am out of the boat now. I cannot turn back... where would I go if not to you? I have to continue to come to you across the waters of my life.

Lord, help me to keep my eyes firmly fixed on you. Help me to ignore life's storms that are raging all around me.

But Lord, if I do take fright and start to sink, let me call to you in my need. I know, Lord, that in your great mercy you will rescue me. I know, Lord, you will never let me sink, how could you, when you love me as you do?

Jesus, I love you, I praise you and I worship you! Jesus, I put my trust in you.

Further Meditation

How much do you trust Jesus when the storm is raging against you?

_____

_____

_____

_____

_____

_____

_____

_____

_____

_____

Listen and reflect on what Jesus is saying to you ...

_____

_____

_____

_____

_____

_____

_____

_____

_____

_____

_____

Seeking and Granting Forgiveness

Then Peter came to Jesus and asked, "Lord how many times shall I forgive my brother or sister who sins against me? Up to seven times?" Jesus answered, "Not seven, I tell you, but seventy times seven".

MATTHEW 18:21-22

... and from The Lord's Prayer ...

Forgive us our debts as we also have forgiven our debtors...
For if you forgive other people when they sin against you, your heavenly Father will also forgive you. But if you do not forgive others their sins, your Father will not forgive your sins.

MATTHEW 6:12, 14-15

Jesus' teaching on forgiveness was truly radical for his time. When Peter asked Jesus whether he should forgive others up to seven times, I think he felt he was on fairly solid ground; after-all the number seven in scripture is the number of completion or perfection. He may also have been thinking of Proverbs 24:16 ... *for though the righteous fall seven times, they rise again.* Yet Jesus answered, not seven but seventy times seven. Jesus actually meant that we are to forgive others an infinite number of times. He was raising the bar of The Mosaic Law. The Old Covenant was based on justice, but the New Covenant was to be based on mercy—doing unto others as you would have them do unto.[12]

Did you notice the last two lines immediately after the Lord's Prayer? *"For if you forgive other people when they sin against you, your heavenly Father will also forgive you. But if you do not forgive others their sins, your Father will not forgive your sins"*. These sentences may surprise you, as they did a young man I was counseling recently. He could not believe these words were in the Bible and checked carefully to see which version I was using. I must admit that I said this prayer for years, without paying attention to these last two lines. I would recite the words "forgive us our trespasses as we forgive those who trespass against us" but somehow just skipped over them. Perhaps it was the memorized repetition of the prayer that allowed me to miss the importance of this message.

When I finally understood this God principle I knew that I had to ask for forgiveness from those who I had wronged, especially my family. So I went to each of my sons and asked them to forgive me for some of the ways I treated them as they were growing up, for example, I was sometimes hard on them, pushing them to be more like me. I think they were genuinely surprised by my words, but we had a heartfelt discussion and I now have an excellent relationship with all of them. I also had to apologize to my wife for the many, many times that I had offended her.

In addition I realized that when I kept bringing up the past against people, even in my mind, I had not really forgiven

12   Luke 6:31

them. I could spend hours going over past hurts in my mind and proving without a shadow of doubt that I was right and my offenders were wrong. I would imagine that I was a High Court judge, sifting all the evidence and then pronouncing a guilty judgment against them. But that isn't forgiveness—it's pride. Don't we all know people who have been so full of anger and bitterness towards others that it has ruined their health, relationships and even their life? What about yourself, are you free from judgment of others?

Forgiveness is one of the keys to our physical, emotional and spiritual healing. A team and I were once praying for physical healing with a man from Iraq who had one leg amputated with a sword by Saddam Hussein's Republican Guard. During the prayer, one of the prayer team asked him if he was able to forgive those who mistreated him in this way; when he did this he was immediately healed from the chronic pain he was still experiencing. He left the church walking limp-free and jumping with joy, something he was unable to do before. Jesus himself set us this example on the cross when he said *"Father, forgive them; for they know not what they do" (Luke 23:34).*

Before we move on, I should add that face to face forgiveness is not necessary if it would place you in danger of further emotional, physical or sexual abuse. If this is the case, you should simply forgive this person from your heart and ask God to bless them and bring them to a place of sorrow and repentance for the harm they have done to you.

Understand that forgiveness is a choice we make. As we let our so-called enemies "off the hook", we become free. We are not condoning what they have done, or forcing ourselves to be

OK with it. They may have been very hurtful to us, but by our free choice, we forgive them, releasing them from the debt they owe us. As we forgive them, we are healed in mind and spirit. Someone once said that unforgiveness is like drinking a cup of poison and expecting the other person to die. We need to forgive others not only for their benefit but for ours. Forgiveness is the key to our peace and inner healing. It is your gift to God and to yourself.

For further reading on this subject I strongly recommend John and Carol Arnott's book *Grace and Forgiveness*.[13] It is a very simple yet profound message and it may just change your life!

I invite you to pray this prayer of forgiveness, recalling those people you would like forgive.

Father, I come to you acknowledging my need of you. I want to give gifts of forgiveness to those who have offended me.

Father I choose to forgive those who have hurt me and sinned against me. What they did was wrong, but I freely choose to do this because you have taught me to forgive, unconditionally, just as Jesus forgave those who crucified Him.

I forgive my father … my mother … my brothers … my sisters … my uncles & aunts and all my relatives … I forgive my husband … my wife … my employers … my priests & pastors … my friends and everyone who has sinned against me.

(Pause and name specifically any person who comes to mind)

---

13   John and Carol Arnott, Grace and Forgiveness, Catch The Fire Books, 2015.

I give them the gift of unconditional forgiveness, with no strings attached, and I ask you to bless them in every way.

Father, I now want to confess my own sins of unforgiveness. I have judged others in bitterness and anger and I want to be free of this. Forgive me Father for dishonoring others in this way.

Father I also ask your forgiveness for the times that I have judged you or blamed you for those things that have gone wrong in my life. Forgive me Lord.

I forgive myself for my own failures. For the many, many times that I have fallen flat on my face, and for thinking of myself as being worthless and having no value. I now realize that I have infinite value in your eyes, and that You love me, unconditionally.

Father, I want to be free of everything that is holding me back from doing your perfect will. I come humbly to you, like the prodigal son to receive your forgiveness. I ask you to restore my inheritance in you and allow me to rest in your arms of love and mercy.

I ask this prayer in Jesus name.

Further Meditation

Are there any people whom you should forgive?

_____

_____

_____

_____

_____

_____

_____

_____

_____

_____

Ask God to give you the grace to forgive them, and where possible, seek reconciliation.

_____

_____

_____

_____

_____

_____

_____

_____

_____

_____

Finding Courage

David said to the Philistine, "You come against me with sword and spear and javelin, but I come against you in the name of the LORD Almighty, the God of the armies of Israel, whom you have defied. This day the LORD will deliver you into my hands..."

1 SAMUEL 17:45-46

And the whole world will know that it is not by sword or spear that the LORD saves; for the battle is the LORD's, and he will give all of you into our hands.

1 SAMUEL 17:47

This scripture passage tells the story of David and Goliath. You may wish to read the whole story in 1 Samuel 17:1-55. David's courage becomes even clearer when you consider the full context of the story.

David was a teenage shepherd boy who found the courage and strength to do what no other soldier in King Saul's army could do—stand up against an oversized bully. How did he do this? Well, while everyone else was focusing on Goliath, David was focusing on God, and his God was much bigger than Goliath. I like to imagine that as David was looking at Goliath, this giant bully, he could see The Lord standing behind Goliath, twice his size and towering over him.

I could have used some of this courage in my childhood

days. Growing up during World War II and experiencing the London blitz, I became a very fearful child and would run away and hide at the first sign of bullying. Luckily I had a big brother who was a lot tougher that I was, and I would rely on him to do my fighting for me. This shyness remained with me into adulthood, even into my late twenties. I remember attending a business training seminar which involved small group discussions, and being taken aside by one of the facilitators and told that I was acting as a spectator and not contributing to the group. I realized that, while I had a lot to add to the conversation, I was lacking the courage to speak up and express my opinion. This was a big wake-up call for me.

David did not rely on human resources such as King Saul's armour and sword. Instead he relied on the skills and resources that God had provided for him; his shepherds' slingshot and his wits. Furthermore he did not listen to all the negative words spoken to him, or take time to calculate the risks and devise a complicated battle plan—he had no Plan B. Instead, he simply trusted in God and acted. Do I trust that God will protect me when the deck seems stacked against me? Not always, but I'm learning! How about you?

Let me tell you about a dream I had, some years ago, about trusting in God's provision. In this dream I was standing at the edge of a deep canyon, like the Grand Canyon in Arizona. There was a small bridge in front of me jutting out over the canyon, but it was unfinished and ended in mid-air. In my spirit I felt that I was meant to step onto it, and as I did a second section of the bridge appeared. This was a very scary feeling, as I tried not to look down into the chasm below.

As I continued to walk forward new bridge spans materialized, until I reached the other side. When I awoke I asked the Lord what the dream meant. I heard "Now you know what trust is all about." Often the purpose of God-dreams is to prepare you for what lies ahead. It wasn't long before I needed to apply this lesson of courage and trust in my life practically!

It happened at a workshop that I was giving to the Order of St. Luke The Physician, on healing prayer. We were in a downtown Toronto church and there were about 60 people in attendance. After a brief talk, and to demonstrate the power of healing prayer, I asked whether anyone would come forward for prayer so that our team could pray for them. A lady sitting in the front pew cried out "Me! Me!" and struggled to her feet. She slowly approached, walking to the podium with the aid of two canes and it was evident that she was severely disabled. I looked up to heaven and thought, "Oh no Lord, you have to be kidding—not in front of all these people, surely." You see, even though I had seen God heal many people in the previous year, this was the first time I was praying for someone in front of a crowd of people—and it was definitely scary! Then I remembered the bridge across the canyon and realized this was not about me, it was about courage and trust in God. So we started to pray and after three or four minutes the lady straightened right up and cried, "I'm healed!" Then she walked quickly up and down the church aisle without pain, something she had not done in years. This happened in the morning session and I saw her later that evening, as she gave her healing testimony, still walking pain-free and without canes. God is so good! You can read a lot more about Healing Prayer on Days 34 to 38.

I think we all have our Goliaths to fight in our lives, and as you are fighting yours I encourage you to remember that you have a great big God on your side. So call on Him with all the strength and courage you can muster and see what He can do!

Let's pray:

O Lord of Hosts, let me always be aware of your presence in my life, in the good times and the hard times. Let me not be discouraged when things seem to be difficult, but rather, let me see you as so much bigger than my problems, and turn to you for help.

Lord, teach me your will so that I may always walk in your ways. Help me to recognize and use the resources that you have provided for me, increase my courage! Lord if you are with me, who can prevail against me?

Lord, give me the strength to do what is right. To protect the weak and the innocent, to comfort those who are in need, to forgive those who have sinned against me, to love others as you have loved me, to be generous as I share the gifts you have given me. And to trust in you, always. I ask all of this in the name of Jesus. Amen.

Further Meditation

Think of a time when you trusted God, and he answered your prayer.

_____

_____

_____

_____

_____

_____

_____

Think of a time when you made a major decision that was not in God's will.

_____

_____

_____

_____

_____

_____

_____

What can you learn from these experiences?

_____

_____

_____

_____

_____

_____

_____

Transformed by the Holy Spirit

I baptize you with the water of repentance, but the one who follows me is more powerful than I am, and I am not fit to carry his sandals; he will baptize you with the Holy Spirit and with fire.

MATTHEW 3:11

When the day of Pentecost came, they were all together in one place. Suddenly a sound like the blowing of a violent wind came from heaven and filled the whole house where they were sitting. They saw what seemed to be tongues of fire that separated and came to rest on each of them. All of them were filled with the Holy Spirit and began to speak in other tongues as the spirit enabled them.

ACTS 2:1-4

Being "Spirit filled" or receiving the Baptism (i.e. download) of the Holy Spirit may be a controversial issue, especially in some churches, where it is not widely practiced or understood. I hope that today's reading will help demystify the subject.

I'm deliberately using the word "download" because it's a non-religious term that accurately describes how God can enter our life and deposit His gifts into our spirit, supernaturally. These days we are familiar with downloading music, videos and apps from the Internet onto our phones, computers and other devices. I don't know how it all works; I just know that it does. Now consider for a moment that is able to download His Spirit into us, whenever He chooses. He invented downloading.

For the first three or four centuries of the early Christian Church, adult Spirit-filled Baptism was standard practice. At this time the special gifts of the Spirit, such as healing, prophecy and tongues, were both anticipated and received. In fact, scholars agree that these Holy Spirit gifts and the signs and miracles that resulted from them were largely responsible for the rapid growth of the early Church. Regrettably, over time, these special gifts of the Holy Spirit were set aside. Apart from occasional waves of revival they have remained forgotten and largely unused. For an excellent review of this subject, I recommend *The Healing Reawakening* by Francis MacNutt.[14]

Let me give you more details of my journey and encounters (downloads) with The Holy Spirit. Until my early 30's I attended church most Sundays, and tried to live a good life. I thought I was fine spiritually but I didn't have a personal relationship with Jesus. I knew about God but I did not have a close relationship with Him. It was rather like "knowing" the Queen of England, without ever having met her in person. Then in the early 1970's, a friend invited me to attend a Catholic Cursillo retreat. Cursillo is a Spanish word that means short course (in Christianity). I didn't really want to go and declined several times; but he was persistent and eventually I agreed to go.

The weekend consisted of a series of talks by men in the congregation followed by small group discussion. I was not accustomed to men talking about their spirituality with such

---

14 Francis MacNutt, The Healing Reawakening, Chosen Books, 2005.

depth and enthusiasm. I particularly remember a humble farmer weeping as he spoke about his relationship with Jesus; I was deeply moved and wondered what I was missing. The first evening was difficult for me, as it focused on knowing yourself - not something I was particularly good at. The next day was a "what" day. What is life all about? What is God all about? What is church all about, and finally, what is Christian living all about? The following day was a "how" day and dealt with topics such as how to live out our daily life, at home, at work, in my community and in my church. The final talk was a wrap-up of what we had learned and prepared us to return to our daily lives.

This weekend wasn't about gaining knowledge or more information about the church, it was experiencing Christian community in action. We enjoyed the support of the outside community as they cooked all of our meals and cleaned up after us. We received personal letters from family, friends and complete strangers telling us of their love and support. This was an experience of church that I had never had before—it was God's love being poured out for us.

There was also the ongoing community. This renewal movement held regular follow-up meetings, which both my wife and I attended; later we went through training and became team members at subsequent weekends. I joined a men's small group that met once a week to share our spiritual journey and to support each other in dealing with the highs and lows of daily living. I found that when I was feeling positive I was able to encourage those who were struggling and when I was down, they were able to help me. I had discovered God at work in the everyday experiences of life.

Then, in the early 1990's, I found myself drawn to a Charismatic prayer group and this is where I received another special download from the Holy Spirit, known as the Baptism in the Spirit. The Greek word used for baptism is *baptizo* which means to saturate with water, as in the image of waterlogged timbers of a sunken ship. Another example might be that of a small cucumber that is pickled with vinegar and spices. Its flavor and texture are permanently transformed—you can never "unpickle" a pickle. That's what it's like to be baptized (pickled) in The Holy Spirit. Can you imagine a notice in your church bulletin announcing "On Sunday we will have a service to get pickled in the Holy Spirit"; that would raise a few eyebrows, wouldn't it?

I received my pickling at a Catholic charismatic conference in Hamilton, Ontario. It occurred during the very first session as I was simply standing by myself and enjoying the worship music. I sensed the presence of God in a totally new way. I felt my hands being drawn up to the ceiling in praise as tears of joy streamed down my face. This was quite extraordinary for me because prior to this experience I was uncomfortable raising my hands during worship. Then I started to babble in some child-like language; something else that I had never done before. I knew that what I was experiencing was not of my own making. I did not ask for anything, I did not call it down. Something just came from the outside in. I knew that it was God pouring His love into me, in a new and very special way. It was if I had received my own personal Pentecost experience, just as the apostles experienced in Acts chapter 2.

Scripture tells us that the presence of God will produce

good fruit in us.[15] So, what are some of the fruits that I have seen in my life?

First, I felt a tremendous love for God. In the beginning, I was overcome by the Holy Spirit and by His love and power. Later, I developed a deep and personal relationship with Jesus as Lord and also as a brother. Finally, Jesus and the Holy Spirit took me to the Father, to my Daddy in Heaven. I have sat on my Father's knee, felt His love for me burn into my heart and I have danced with Him *"on the streets that are golden"*.[16] I know how much God loves me, and this love has transformed my life.

During this time I also developed a great love for scripture. Prior to this time I hardly ever read the Bible, but then God's Word came alive for me. I was able to read both the New and Old Testament and place myself into the narrative. Rather than being historical, the message was current and alive. I hope these pages bear witness to this fact. Today I lead a weekly Bible teaching in a Christian drop-in centre close to where I live.

So how does one go about receiving the Baptism in the Spirit? As you can see from my testimony it can be both a sudden and an ongoing process. To begin with, there are many different seminars that you can attend to learn about and receive this special grace; "Life in the Spirit", "The Alpha Program" and "Abundant Life" series, to name just a few. In some churches it is normal to have elders or other leaders pray over you for the Baptism in the Holy Spirit. In other churches it is

15   Mat 3:8; 7:17; 12:33. John 15:5. Rom 7:4. Gal 5:22
16   Rev 21:21

mostly left up to God to decide when and how His anointing will occur. However you receive these gifts, I strongly recommend that you become an active member of a Spirit-filled community and accept the guidance of mature people. This is the best way to learn how to use your spiritual gifts wisely. As stated in 1 Corinthians 12, these gifts are for the benefit of the church at large, so if you want to keep them you will have to learn how to use them in the service of others. This learning process will, like other experiences, often be a matter of learning from your mistakes. Many of the following readings will describe these gifts in more detail.

If you wish to pray for the Baptism in the Holy Spirit, here is a prayer you can use. It would be best to pray this prayer in the presence of another believer or prayer partner.

Father, I acknowledge that I have sinned against you and against my neighbour. I am sorry for my sins and ask for your forgiveness. I acknowledge that Jesus died on the cross for me, and by His death and resurrection I am redeemed.

Jesus, I now invite you to take your place on the throne of my life. To be the centre of my life. My all in all.

Fill me with the Holy Spirit as you promised in your Word.[17] Fill me with your love. Fill me with your fire. Baptize me with your Holy Spirit.

---

17   John 16:7

Direct my steps to a place where I can learn more about you, and where I can grow and be a blessing to you and to the church.

I ask this prayer in Jesus' Holy name. Amen.

Further Meditation

Did you pray this prayer? Then allow yourself to rest and quietly sense what the Spirit is saying to you.

_____

_____

_____

_____

_____

_____

_____

_____

What action can you take to find a Spirit-filled community near you?

_____

_____

_____

_____

_____

_____

_____

_____

Hearing From God

Incline your ear, and come to Me. Hear, and your soul shall live.

ISAIAH 55:3 NKJV

My sheep hear My voice, and I know them, and they follow Me.

JOHN 10:27

Are you thinking "I've never heard God speaking to me?" If you're saying this to yourself I assure you that you are not alone; in fact you are probably in the majority of Christians. Yet God has promised that He will speak with us and that we will hear His voice. Why can't we hear his voice? In truth, I believe that we all hear God speaking to us; it's just that we don't recognize that it is Him. When we say "hearing" from God, we don't have to hear with our ears; mostly we hear with our hearts. Have you ever felt prompted by God to do, or not do, something? Well then, you have heard God speak to you!

I remember one of the first times I heard God speak to me, not in an audible voice, but deep in my heart. I was a teenager at the time and my parents, brother and I were on vacation in Germany. One day we went to the city of Cologne and visited the Catholic cathedral, which dominated the city centre. It's the largest cathedral in northern Europe and dates back to the 1200's, although it was not completed until much later. It was badly damaged during the war, but repaired in the 1950's.

As I stood and looked up to the vaulted ceiling, I couldn't help but imagine how during the war this church would have been filled with German citizens praying for peace and victory. And then I thought of all the English churches that at that same time would also have been filled with people praying for peace and victory. I remember asking God what He thought about the contradiction of two nations at war, both praying for victory over each other. That's when I heard Him say to my heart, "They are all my children and I love them equally; go and do likewise". This was not what I expected to hear! It was such a profound message that I knew immediately that it was from God, and it changed my thinking forever. I have to confess that as a young boy growing up during the war and experiencing the London Blitz, I didn't have a great love for the German people. But from this moment forward I developed a deep respect and regard for them. I studied German in college, and it's no accident that thirty years later I became president of a Canadian-German joint-venture company.

Much has been written about hearing from God and I believe most authors would agree on the following suggestions to discern his voice:

> » **Set aside time just for listening to God.**
>   Notice that I didn't say talking to God, I said listening to Him. I was brought up with the idea that prayer is talking to God, so I would fill my prayer time with prayers of petition, which is mostly asking God to do things for me. Yet Psalm 139 tells us that God reads our thoughts and knows our words before we say them. So why did

I spend so much time of my prayer talking? Wasn't most of my talking redundant? When I am having a conversation with someone, do I do all the talking then just finish, say "goodbye" and walk away? Of course not! Yet sometimes I wonder if that's how my "Amen" must have sounded to God.

» **Empty your minds of everyday concerns.**
Louis Evely describes this so beautifully in his work, *That Man is You.*[18]

"*A Trappist friend of mine used to say, 'It's not enough to apply the brakes on your car; you must also cut the motor that's racing inside.' The engine of our life is still whirring at top speed. It has to slacken, decelerate and turn at an easier pace. We have to move in time with another rhythm, gear our will to another will, learn to connect with the slow-paced, quiet, powerful and steady motor of God's will.*"

Here are some practical ideas that I found helpful.

» Set aside some time each day, or week, just for listening. No talking—just listening. Find a quiet place for this exercise away from people, TV, your phone, etc. Make this a quality time; it's hard to listen when you are tired, worried or distracted.

» Place yourself in His presence by reading a favourite scripture, or listening to worship music. When you are truly peaceful, set aside your reading or music,

---

18   Louis Everly, That Man is You, Paulist Press Deus Books, 1967.

and ask the Holy Spirit to speak you. Ask Him a simple open-ended question like, "What do you want to say to me?"

» Have paper and pencil available to write down anything that the Lord communicates to you. I describe how to do this in the next reading, on journaling.

How do we know that we are hearing from God and not from our own mind?

» The message should be consistent with scripture, and the character of God.

» It should lead to positive growth in your life.

» It should be accompanied by a sense of peace and release of anxiety.

» It should not be condemning or lead to guilt.

» Often it will come as a surprise and not what you would have thought of for yourself, but it will also feel right for you.

» Finally, if you are in doubt about whether you have heard from God or you own mind, speak with someone you trust, who knows God well, about it.

When I think back more than 50 years to the word I heard in Cologne Cathedral it passes every one of these tests. Isn't it amazing that God can reach into our lives experientially without us having prior teaching or understanding of what is happening? I often remind myself that I should stop trying to organize things so tightly and just let God do things His way.

Let me relate another story about hearing from God. I was

attending a small group meeting from our church and asked
the Holy Spirit if there was another name by which I could call
Him. I wanted a deeper relationship with Him and didn't feel
"The Holy Spirit" was a very user-friendly name. The answer
I heard was "You can call Me Aya." The only other time I had
heard this name was when my youngest son worked at a company called Aya Kitchens, a high-end kitchen cabinet manu-
facture, close to where we lived. So I was inclined to think
that I was listening to my own mind. Somewhat hesitantly I
asked the other members of the group what "AYA" meant to
them. One of them said "in my country it means brother,"
while another commented "where I come from it means "man
of God" hence the term Ayatollah." Later I asked a man from
the Philippines and he said, "it means a care-giver or even a
baby sitter." Finally, I searched on Google and found that in
the Quechan language, spoken in the Amazon region, it means
spirit. In addition Aya (variant spelling Aiah) has a Hebrew
root meaning "a falcon, hawk or vulture" and "to fly swiftly."
It is also a Hebrew unisex name which appears twice in the
Bible; Aiah, the son of Zibeon[19] and Aiah the father of Rizpah.[20]

So I believe there is scriptural support for the name Aya
(Aiah); it has a Hebrew root and is mentioned in the Bible.
The meanings that I was given from friends are also consistent with the caring nature of God (Psalms 23, 91 and 103),
and the supportive nature of the Holy Spirit. It is also in
agreement with Jesus referring to His followers as "brothers"
(Matthew 12:48-50). Let me be clear, I'm not suggesting that

---

19   Genesis 36:24 & 1 Chronicales 1:40
20   2 Samuel 3:7 & 2 Samuel 21:8

Aya is the proper name for the Holy Spirit; I'm simply saying that I believe it is a name by which He said I could call Him; like a nickname between friends, and that it passes the test of hearing God accurately.

To deepen your conversations with God, I recommend reading Mark Virkler's books on Hearing from God,[21,22] or visit his website[23] and view his full range of resources.

Let's pray to better hear God speaking to us:

Lord, My creator and redeemer, I love you. I praise you and give you glory.

Lord, I so want to hear you voice, and to know that it is really you talking to me.

I admit Lord, that in my prayer time I often do most of the talking. I'm sorry for this. Teach me that it is more important that I listen to you, than talk because you already know my concerns before I speak.

Teach me how to still my mind and my thoughts, so that I can come into your presence and listen to you. Let me mean it, sincerely, when I say, "Speak Lord, your servant is listening".[24]

I ask this prayer in Jesus' name. Amen

---

21   Mark & Patty Virkler, 4 Keys to Hearing God's Voice, Destiny Image Publisher, 2010.
22   Mark & Patti Virkler, Hearing God, Destiny Image Publisher, 2014.
23   Mark Virkler's website Communicating with God is cwgministries.org
24   1 Samuel 3:9-10

Further Meditation

Can you think of a time when God has spoken to you, or prompted you to do something?

_____

_____

_____

_____

_____

_____

_____

_____

_____

_____

What impact did it have on your life?

_____

_____

_____

_____

_____

_____

_____

_____

_____

_____

Journaling

*Surely the LORD our God has shown us His glory and His greatness, and
we have heard His voice... We have seen this day that God speaks with man.*

DEUTERONOMY 5:24

*Then the LORD replied: "Write down the revelation and make it plain on
tablets so that a herald may run with it."*

HABAKKUK 2:2

In the above scripture the Lord is telling Habakkuk to record
what God is saying to him so that the message can be dis-
seminated and put to good use. This same guidance applies
to you and me today, we are being asked to write down what
we sense and hear from the Lord. I was introduced to this
concept in a book by Rev. Farrell called *Prayer is a Hunger,*[25] in
which he writes:

*"One way I have learnt to pray is by writing. I began by copying favor-
ite passages from scripture, then the thoughts and ideas of other authors,
and finally jotting down my own insights and reflections from prayer. This
prayer journal at times seems like my own biography of Christ, a kind of
fifth Gospel. There is I hope something of the evangelists' grace for each of us.
What is written is not as significant as what happens to us in the process.*

25 Fr. Edward Farrell, Prayer is a Hunger, Dimensions Book, 1972. Still available
on-line.

Something is growing within; a hidden capacity gently unfolds itself. New sensitivities unfold. A journal is a journey with Christ."

Forty years ago I started journaling exactly as Rev. Farrell described, by copying out prayers that others had written and gradually started to add my own thoughts and prayers. I also added my notes and summaries of Christian books and articles, focusing on those parts that were especially relevant to me. And I found that Rev. Farrell was accurate, a new ability started to unfold and my journal became a journey with Christ. Now, as look back at some of my earlier journals I see how far I have progressed and how God has indeed answered my prayers.

As you start hearing from God and recording what He is saying to you, here are some guidelines that I have found helpful:

Do:

» Be in a spirit of peace and allow the Holy Spirit to guide you.

» Test everything you write against scripture. God will never violate His own truth as already expressed in the Bible. Do this testing after you have finished writing, not as you are in the process. This is important and will avoid you second-guessing yourself as you write.

» If you are not sure whether what you have written is from God or from your own mind, ask a trusted and likeminded person for their opinion. You can

also re-read the checklist[26] in the previous reading.
Receiving confirmation will help you gain confidence and discernment.

» You can also investigate Mark Virkler's websites
cwgministries.org.[27] and bornofthespirit.today[28]

» Be very careful asking God for yes/no decisions
on stressful or emotional issues in your life. If the
issue you are praying for is bigger in your con-
sciousness than the presence of Jesus, it is likely
that your own mind will block out the still, quiet
voice of God.

Don'ts:

» Don't let negative thoughts prevent you from trying
this out. They may try to fill your mind with things
like "This is stupid" or "This will never work for me".
Ignore these negative thoughts; just go for it!

» Don't take any dramatic action, like quitting your
job or moving to another country, without getting
confirmation from another source, such as a close
friend, your pastor or spiritual counselor. Although
he could and has done this before,[29] God will not
likely ask you to move halfway around the world
or take other drastic actions, without confirmation
from other sources.

---

26 How do we know we are hearing from God? Day 15.
27 See Day 15.
28 See Day 6.
29 Abraham, for instance.

Here is a prayer to help you start journaling—have a pen and paper nearby:

Lord I would like to grow and journey with You, and I would like to journal this process. To record what you are saying personally to me. However, I can't do this alone, so please help me.

Show me how to get started. Help me put aside all negative thoughts that this won't work, or that it's not for me.

Lord, even if I am not sure whether I'm hearing you, or from my own mind, let me press forward, what do I have to lose? If it's not helpful I will discard it but if it is from you, I will keep it and treasure it.

Lord, bring people into my life who can help me to grow in you.

Father, I ask this prayer in Jesus name.

Further Meditation

Following the above guidelines, ask God a question and journal His reply.

_____

_____

_____

_____

_____

Here are some suggestions to get started:

_____

_____

_____

_____

_____

"Lord, how do I start?"

_____

_____

_____

_____

"Lord, what do you want to say to me?"

_____

_____

_____

_____

"Lord, do you really love me, despite my sins?"

_____

_____

_____

_____

Putting on the Mind of Christ

... and be renewed in the spirit of your mind that you put on the new man
which was created according to God, in true righteousness and holiness.

EPHESIANS 4:23-24 NKJV

Do not conform to the pattern of this world, but be transformed by the
renewing of your mind. Then you will be able to test and approve what
God's will is—his good, pleasing and perfect will.

ROMANS 12:2

Renew your mind. Change your thinking. Change your behavior. Actively resist Satan by surrendering your mind to God. Does this all seem too difficult? Too radical? It is, when we rely on human means—but in the spiritual realm, all things are possible.

Webster's dictionary lists one of the meanings for the word *dis* as "the god of the lower world, Hades." "Dis" is of course the root of such words as *dis*ease, *dis*comfort, *dis*cord, *dis*order, *dis*allow, *dis*approve, *dis*array, *dis*aster, *dis*believe and many other *dis*agreeable conditions. None of these things were a part of God's original plan for mankind;[30] they are mostly a product of mankind's faulty thinking and cooperation with the evil-one. It's interesting to note that most, if not all, sin starts

---

30 Jeremiah 29:11; John 17:20-22

in the mind. This is where we separate right from wrong and decide what to do, good or bad. It's not surprising that the apostles Paul and James encouraged their followers to renew their minds and change their thinking, and put on the mind of Christ—that is, to think as Christ thinks.

As we look around the world today it is not difficult to see the harm that Satan is causing in the lives' of many people; things like violence, broken marriages, physical, emotional and sexual abuse, addictions and so on—but it doesn't have to be this way. Each one of us can change our life by changing our thinking. It may involve getting rid of the lies we believe about ourselves, about others, and even about God, and replacing them with the truth. We'll look at this further on Days 36 & 37.

Jesus was not kidding when He said *"I am the way and the truth and the life. No one comes to the Father except through me"* (John 14:6).

I hope you will see that this book is a testimony to how my mind was renewed and my thinking changed as a result of my encounters with God. If you want to hear other testimonies, many of them quite remarkable, you may wish to visit iam-second.com. This website is dedicated to stories and videos of how God has changed lives through encounters with Him. You will find videos of people who have dealt with some of life's most difficult issues, under such headings as abortion, abuse, anger, addiction, self-esteem, suicide, the sex trade and war. All of these are examples of the *dis*orders that Satan has sown into our world.

If you are battling with negative thoughts right now and don't know where to turn, I recommend a book by Joyce

Myers called *Battlefield of the Mind*.[31] This no-nonsense book gives you practical advice and biblical concepts to help you get rid of your negative thinking and start thinking with the mind of Christ. Another good Christian book that describes the structure of the brain and how it works to control our body chemistry and emotions is *Who Turned Off My Brain* by Dr. Caroline Leaf.[32] In this book[33] she writes "A massive body of research collectively shows that up to 80% of physical, emotional and mental health issues today could be a direct result of our thought lives. You can break the cycle of toxic thinking and start to build healthy patterns that bring peace to a stormy thought life." She then goes on to give practical tools to aid this process.

Sometimes, when I'm in a Christian bookstore and simply browsing the shelves, a book will catch my eye and practically leap off the shelf for me. I no longer think of these occasions as chance events, I now recognize them as God-moments—opportunities for me to encounter Him and change my thinking.

Let's pray:

Jesus, I need your help. I admit that my thinking is all messed-up. I have believed lies about myself, others and even you Lord, and this has caused major problems in my life.

---

31 Joyce Myers, Battlefield of the Mind, Word Alive, 2002.
32 Dr. Caroline Leaf, Who Turned off my Brain, Thomas Nelson, new edition November 2009. Website drleaf.com
33 Ibid. page 15.

I want to renew my mind and start thinking as you do. To think Your thoughts and to do Your will in my life.

But Lord, I know that this is not possible by my own strength, I need your help. Show me what to do Lord. Guide me to people and places that can help. But above all Lord, keep me close to you.

Father, I ask this prayer in Jesus' Holy Name. Amen

Further Meditation

Would you describe your thought pattern as mostly positive, or mostly negative?

_____
_____
_____
_____
_____
_____

What can you do to change your negative thinking? Resolve to take action.

_____
_____
_____
_____
_____
_____

Waging Spiritual Warfare

Jesus said...He (Satan) was a murderer from the start, he was never grounded in the truth, there is no truth in him at all. When he lies he is drawing on his own store, because he is a liar, and the father of all lies.

JOHN 8:44 JB

Finally, be strong in the Lord and in his mighty power. Put on the full armor of God, so that you can take your stand against the devil's schemes. For our struggle is not against flesh and blood, but against the rulers, against the authorities, against the powers of this dark world and against the spiritual forces of evil in the heavenly realms.

EPHESIANS 6:10-12

In Day 18, I brought up the subject of Satan and some of the evil that is contaminating our world today. While I don't believe it is helpful to focus on Satan or his activities, we need to face the reality that we are living in a fallen world; a world that is frequently influenced by evil. Did you know that Satan was once a powerful angel serving God in Heaven and his name was Lucifer, which means "shining light" or "morning star". But Lucifer wasn't satisfied serving God, he wanted to be like God. In Isaiah chapter 14 (below) we read an account of the fall of the King of Babylon, which Bible scholars tell us also points to the fall of Lucifer.

How you have fallen from heaven, morning star, son of the dawn (Lucifer)!

You have been cast down to the earth, you who once laid low the nations!

You said in your heart, "I will ascend to the heavens; I will raise my throne

above the stars of God; I will sit enthroned on the mount of assembly, on

the farthest side of the north. I will ascend above the tops of the clouds; I

will make myself like the Most High."

ISAIAH 14:12-15

Scripture is full of reference to our encounters with Satan. From Genesis to the Book of Revelation we have accounts of mankind's interaction not only with God, but also with Satan. In fact, if we take Satan out of the Bible, what are we left with? If man had never fallen from God's grace, we would still be *"walking with God in the garden in the cool of the day" (Genesis 3:8).* We would not need the Bible to tell us what God is like; we would know Him for ourselves, personally. The whole purpose of Sacred Scripture is to tell us about man's struggle with evil, and God's redemptive plan. Even Jesus had a direct confrontation with Satan, after He had fasted for forty days in the wilderness.[34]

We also experience temptation, and do things that we know are wrong. When this happens I have found the following approach helpful for myself and I have also used it when counseling others. It's a four-step process:

1. Recognize that you are experiencing a temptation from the devil.

34   Matthew 4:1-11

As I mentioned in Day 18, most temptation starts in the mind and therefore overcoming temptation begins in the mind as well. Try to realize that what you are feeling or experiencing is from the devil. Every great saint, and even Jesus himself, underwent temptation. Even experiencing a strong temptation does not mean that you are a bad person. One of Satan's tactics is to tempt you to sin and then make you feel guilty about it afterwards. If he can keep you wallowing in feelings of shame and guilt, then you are less likely to fix the problem. Temptations are not sinful in themselves, it's what you do about them that determines whether you offend God or not.

2. Turn away from evil and toward Jesus.

Make the conscious decision that you want to resist this temptation, because you know it's not God's will for you. Turn away from it as soon as you recognize the situation. Do your best not to entertain negative thoughts, bitterness, sexual fantasies or other thinking that leads you to sin. Then invite Jesus into these dark areas of your life. As you turn your back on this temptation, I find that visualization often helps. If you see yourself as if you are at a crossroad, then you have to ability in your mind to turn your back on the temptation and turn towards Jesus. Ask for His help in this act of repositioning your will.

3. Casting off the evil spirit

Whenever possible, it helps to recognize the evil spirit responsible for your temptation, for example, the spirit of anger, spirit of lust, spirit of addiction, spirit of loneliness, spirit of confusion, etc. Try to mentally visualize this spirit as something nasty and evil (perhaps as a little red devil) and say this prayer to it, directly and out loud:[35]

Prayer:

Spirit of (name it), *I turn away from you and I turn towards Jesus. I want nothing to do with you. In the name of Jesus, I command you to depart from me now. You have no authority over me; you have no power over me. I am a child of Jesus and in the name of Jesus I command you be gone, be gone, be gone.*

Repeat this prayer with faith and conviction until you feel calmness in your spirit.

4. Giving thanks and praise to God

Try to finish the previous prayer with an attitude of thanksgiving to God. Thank Him for your salvation and all the blessings He has placed in your life. I suggest reading your favourite passage of scripture or playing worship music.

You should note that temptation may return to you again and again, particularly those associated with long-term sin. If this occurs you may need to repeat the above steps again and again. As you experience success with this prayer, your confidence will increase and gradually the temptations will lessen. If, after some time you are not successful, seek healing

---

35   Note there is more on temptation and evil spirits in Day 31, Deliverance.

prayer or prayer counseling from an experienced ministry. It may be that you need inner healing or deliverance prayer; see Days 36 to 38 to learn more. But have faith that the Holy Spirit will guide you to victory in this battle. It is God's will that you prevail! You will be victorious!

Prayer to fight repeated temptations:

Lord, I'm tired of struggling against this (name it) *temptation. I have tried so many times to resist, but I just can't shake it.*

Teach me to recognize Satan's lies that I have believed about myself and about others. Teach me how to regain my heritage in you O God as a child of God, your child, Abba, Father.

Lord, I come now to you for help. You know my inner secrets and my inner needs. You have been with me since my conception and have already rescued me from so many trials and tribulations.

Show me Lord how I can finally overcome this temptation, send your Holy Spirit to lead me in prayer.

And Lord if I do need extra help in getting to the root cause of my problem, then direct my steps to whatever ministry or counselor I need. I ask this in the name of Jesus. Amen

Further Meditation

Are their areas in your life that you need God's help to improve?

_____

_____

_____

_____

_____

_____

_____

_____

_____

_____

_____

Resolve, right now, that you will seek help; to whom can you turn?

_____

_____

_____

_____

_____

_____

_____

_____

_____

_____

_____

_____

Understanding the Law of Reaping and Sowing

Whoever sows injustice reaps calamity, and the rod they wield in fury will

be broken.

PROVERBS 22:8

Do not be deceived: God cannot be mocked. A man reaps what he sows.

Whoever sows to please their flesh, from the flesh will reap destruction;

whoever sows to please the Spirit, from the Spirit will reap eternal life.

GALATIANS 6:7

Oh dear, scripture says that whatever I sow, I reap. In other words, if I sow good things I reap goodness, but if I do bad stuff, it will come back to haunt me. And as I look back on my life now, I can see that it is true. I have benefited greatly from the good things that I have done, but just as surely, I have experienced suffering from the wrongs that I have done. If I had to live my life over again there are lots of mistakes that I would try to avoid. Mostly, I would try to behave differently towards the people I love, especially my family and friends. I would try to be more loving, more compassionate, more understanding—more Christ-like.

I'm also conscious of the effects of reaping and sowing as I counsel others, particularly the men in the correctional institution where I volunteer. I see how the bad things they have done earlier in life have caused havoc later on. I see marriages and careers ruined, parents too ashamed to acknowledge their children, health severely damaged, and more.

Let me tell you the true story of a young man, whom I'll call Kevin, who came from one of the toughest neighbourhoods in Toronto. He came from a violent home and was brought up by his mother after his parents divorced when he was six years old. By the time he was twelve he was taking drugs and getting into fights at school. He developed a toughboy attitude; he carried a weapon and acted like a gangster. By age sixteen he had been expelled from two schools, and placed in a foster home because his mother could no longer handle him. He drifted from one bad situation to another, and his weapon of choice escalated from his fists to a knife, to a machete and then to a .22 caliber handgun. He joined one of the more violent street gangs in the city and his criminal acts worsened to include drug offences, robbery, and assaults, for which he was arrested and jailed several times.

Kevin was in his late twenties when he finally realized that his life was a total mess. He had been arrested again for a violent robbery in which someone was injured. He was found guilty and given a relatively light sentence of four years, some of which had to be served in a Correctional/Rehabilitation Facility.

Because of his record, Kevin was initially sent to a maximum security prison before being transferred to the Correctional Facility. It was in the maximum security jail that he noticed a group of inmates reading and studying together, led by an older inmate I'll call David. Kevin asked David what they were doing. David replied that they were learning about the Bible and asked whether he wanted to join their group. Kevin's grandmother was a Christian and had told him something about Jesus when he was a child, but he had never become involved in church.

There was something about David's character that captivated Kevin and he guardedly agreed to sit in on one of the sessions. Gradually David became a mentor to him, demonstrating a love, gentleness, and wisdom that he had never imagined or experienced before. David became the father that Kevin never had. Kevin began to read the Bible and absorb the message of God's love and forgiveness. Then one night as he lay in bed Kevin prayed the first real prayer of his life. It went something like this, "God, if you're real, I need your help. I can't go on like this anymore, I can't do it alone. Please help." With that he felt a tremendous peace come upon him. This peace remained with him for days and he felt an incredible hunger for learning more about God. He became like a sponge, absorbing everything he could; he was not seeking religion, he was seeking God. Sometime later Kevin accepted Jesus into his life and David baptized him with a cup of water in the prison washroom.

When Kevin told me this story I was captivated by the peace that radiated from his face. It was hard to imagine that the serene man sitting across from me had led the violent life that he had just described. He had experienced a complete transformation that no amount of professional counseling or treatment could have achieved. I say this with experience, having counseled, with varied success, a number of inmates over the years—from sex offenders to drug dealers. So I am not easily deceived by someone trying to fake it. Kevin's transformation is for real, and it all started with a desperate cry for help.

Kevin and I now have weekly meetings; we don't just talk about God, but also about living a useful and productive life when he is released. He has a girlfriend who has stuck by him and they are planning to get married as soon as possible. He has already written his story in much greater detail than I have given here, and hopes that one day he can share his story with other young people, to keep them out of trouble and bring them to Christ.

For me, it's always wonderful to see people commit their lives to Jesus in church, but I find it even more exciting when God accomplishes this inside a maximum security prison. Indeed, scripture tells us that Jesus did not come for the righteous or holy people, but for the sinners.[36]

When you consider Kevin's story you can see how his violent behavior led to jail, repentance, and then redemption. Although this situation may be extreme, you may be aware of things you've done and choices that you've made that have hurt others and even yourself. We can't change the past, but with God's help we can affect the future. If that's you, I invite you to pray the following prayer:

Lord Jesus, I admit I have behaved badly in the past. (Take a moment to recall anything that comes to mind ...)

Lord, I am sorry for my sin, I confess that what I did was wrong, I ask

36 Mark 2:17

for your forgiveness. Jesus, I accept you as my Lord and Saviour. Come into my heart today.

Lord, come into this situation today and remove the effects that are still lingering in my life. Teach me how to sow blessings, not harm. And heal others whom I have hurt.

Lord, I want to set out on a new path, right now, a path of peace, love, and grace.

Show me your way, Lord. Help me by sending your Holy Spirit to guide and support me. With your help, your grace, all things are possible. Thank you Jesus for answering this prayer. Amen.

Further Meditation

Can you see how the message of sowing and reaping is true in your life? What good seed have you sown?

_____
_____
_____
_____

What bad seed would you like to make amends for? Ask God to help.

_____
_____
_____
_____

Proclaiming God's Word:
Personal Prophecy

Follow the way of love and eagerly desire gifts of the Spirit, especially prophecy the one who prophesies speaks to people. ... the one who prophesies speaks to people for their strengthening, encouraging and comfort.

1 CORINTHIANS 14:1, 3

Never try to suppress the Spirit, or to treat the gift of prophecy with contempt, think before you do anything, hold on to what is good, and avoid every form of evil.

1 THESSALONIANS 5:19

Prophecy is one of the spiritual gifts spoken about in 1 Corinthians chapters 12 through 14 and it can be defined as "speaking forth God's word". Growing up in a more traditional church, I was familiar with the Old Testament prophets such as Isaiah, Ezekiel and Daniel, but I knew nothing about prophecy in light of the New Testament and the gifts of the Holy Spirit. I sometimes wondered whether we still had prophets in the church today, and if so, what was their role? Well, through personal experience and sound biblical teaching, I am now satisfied that the answer is an emphatic YES; furthermore the prophet's role today is exactly the same as it always has been. Paraphrasing from 1 Corinthians 14:3 above, the role of the prophet is to lift up, build up and cheer up the people of God. The prophet is also used by the Holy Spirit to foretell of future God-events and, on occasion, give correction to those who are acting against God's will.

There are several different kinds of prophecy. Today I will focus on personal prophecy; that is prophecy intended for an individual. On Day 22, we will look at corporate prophecy; that is prophecy intended for a whole community.

Personal Prophecy:

Let me illustrate this with an example. More than ten years ago some friends and I attended a four-day prophetic conference at my church in Toronto.[37] This was a large conference with over two thousand participants, representing almost every Christian denomination and country in the world. It was truly an amazing gathering of God's people.

At the end of the first evening, as we were on the way home, my car developed an electrical fault and broke down. It was almost midnight as I pulled off the highway and called for a tow truck to haul the car to a local garage. Not a good way to end the day! The next morning my son drove me to the conference, just in time for the first session. After a teaching on prophecy, the leader asked each person to pair off with someone they did not know, and I found myself partnered with a very tall Norwegian gentleman. After brief introductions we were asked to pray a blessing over one another, as the Holy Spirit led us. My partner started to pray over me in the Spirit

---

37   In all future references "my church" or "my home church" refers to Catch The Fire Toronto, formerly known as Toronto Airport Christian Fellowship.

and then, after a short time stopped and said, "Michael, do you own a car?" I said yes, and then he continued, "I feel really silly saying this, but I believe the Lord wants me to pray about your car. God wants you to know that He loves you unconditionally and that this includes your possessions, even your car. He will take care of your car."

I was blown away! God sent this complete stranger, from halfway across the world, to tell me He cares about my old, broken-down car. This was truly a pivotal moment for me. It spoke volumes about the love of God, but it also seemed to release my own prophetic gifts. From that moment on, I had all the proof I needed that today God still speaks to his people in prophecy.

I have also received several prophetic words concerning this book over the years. First the word spoken more than fifteen years ago that God wanted me to write a book, as I shared in the Introduction. Then in 2011, a prophet whom I had never met came to our church and spoke these words over me. "Michael, you have rich experience with the Lord, and many stories to tell. You will have greater authority to speak with this experience, to encourage others to move forward. You have many stories to share with those you counsel." I believe this word applies to the stories I share in this book, and it has has been a great encouragement to me. I don't know that I would have kept going with this project without the sure knowledge that it was God's idea, not mine.

A habit that I have developed over the years is to write down all the prophetic words that reliable prophets speak into my life. These days it's even easier to record these words on my smartphone. During times of discouragement I find it really helps to re-read or re-play these words and gain new strength and encouragement from them. I also have to remind myself to be patient, as there is often a period of time between when I receive a word and when it is fulfilled—sometimes months, sometimes years, sometimes decades.

Word of Knowledge:

A Word of Knowledge is a word from God about another person or situation, which is intended to benefit the receiver. Again, let me illustrate this point with an example. I typically receive Words of Knowledge when ministering to other people. Once, the Lord showed me that a woman whom I was praying with needed to forgive her brother for something that had happened when they were both children. This incident was sexual in nature, certainly not something I felt comfortable raising in conversation with her. In fact, for a moment I thought, "Oh no Lord, I'm not going there!" But later I prayed and asked the Lord, "If you really want something done about this, let her bring up the subject, in her own time."

At a subsequent meeting, she mentioned something about her brother. I commented that she had never mentioned her brother before, and asked her to tell me about him. As she talked about him there came a point in our conversation when I was able to very gently inquire whether, when they were children, there had been any sort of improper contact between them. She paused, for the longest time, and then said yes. Then I was able to relate what the Lord had revealed to me, and asked if she was willing to forgive him. Again, she said yes.

Later she met privately with her brother, forgave him face to face and there was much weeping and reconciliation between them. Would this have happened without God's intervention? I doubt it.

Healing evangelists usually rely on Words of Knowledge for their ministries. Whether they are on stage in a crowded public meeting or privately meeting with someone, they sense what the Lord wants to do, speak out what they are hearing, and let God do the rest. Indeed, even Jesus relied on Words of Knowledge from His Father throughout his earthly ministry.[38]

But how can we be sure that a prophetic Word really does come from God, and not from a person's mind?

It's very important that we are not deceived by false prophets, and that we are able to distinguish between God's Word and human words. So here are some accepted guidelines that many spiritual leaders use to test prophetic words.

- » Prophecy must conform to scripture. The Holy Spirit is a Spirit of order and will always agree with his previous revelations in the Bible.
- » In order to apply to you, the word must ring true to your spirit. It will never advise you to do something you know to be wrong, but it can stretch you into greater faith or even correct you in your life's path.
- » The prophecy must bear good fruit in your life, although this may take time to become evident. It is a principle of scripture that a tree is judged by

---

38   John 6:38, John 14:10-11

its fruit.[39] If the word is from God, it will benefit you or another person.

» It's often appropriate to wait on the Lord for confirmation of a prophecy. Knowing what God wants does not automatically give us the power, or authority to act. There is frequently a period of time between a word and its fulfillment. God always finds a way to give confirmation of His word if it is needed; this often occurs through another person when the time is right.

» When both the message and timing are clear then it is time to act. It is good to have others pray about your word, and speak into your life; there is wisdom in the counsel of many. God will reward you when you step out in faith.

Let's pray for greater revelation of God's word in our lives:

Holy Spirit, please speak your prophetic word into my life. Words of love, encouragement and hope. Help me know with absolute certainty, that it is You speaking to me. And lead me to others who will teach me more about your prophetic gifts and hearing your voice.

Give me confirmation of your Word, at the appropriate time, so that I will move forward with courage and confidence to complete what you have spoken for me.

I ask this in Jesus name. Amen

---

39   Luke 6:43-45

Further Meditation

Have you ever had prophetic words spoken over you that have already been fulfilled?

_____

_____

_____

_____

_____

_____

_____

_____

_____

_____

_____

Have you given up on words that have not yet been fulfilled? Is so, pray for guidance regarding God's will for this situation.

_____

_____

_____

_____

_____

_____

_____

_____

_____

_____

_____

Proclaiming God's Word: Corporate Prophecy

As the rain and the snow come down from heaven, and do not return to it without watering the earth and making it bud and flourish, so that it yields seed for the sower and bread for the eater, so is my word that goes out from my mouth: It will not return to me empty, but will accomplish what I desire and achieve the purpose for which I sent it.

ISAIAH 55:10-11

Now I wish that you all might speak in tongues, but more especially to prophesy, since the one who prophesies is greater (of more importance) than the one who speaks in tongues...

1 CORINTHIANS 14:5 AMP

Corporate Prophecy:

Corporate Word is prophecy spoken over a group of people, a church, a city or even a nation.

In May 1992, for example, Marc DuPont, a leading prophet from the U.S., had the following vision concerning Toronto, Canada. Here is a brief excerpt of what he recorded:[40]

"I had a vision of water falling over and onto an extremely large rock.

---

40   Jerry Steingard with John Arnott, From Here to the Nations, Catch The Fire Books, 2014 page 38.

The amount of water was similar to Niagara Falls. Toronto shall be a place where much living water will be flowing with great power ... There will be a radical move in late '93 throughout '94 ... Like Jerusalem, Toronto will end up being a sending out place. It is of God that there are so many internationals in this area. The Lord is going to send out many people, filled with His Spirit with strong gifting, vision, and love to the nations on all continents. There are going to be new Bible Schools, training centres, and leadership schools raised up in the move that is coming. These schools will have a focus not only on Bible Knowledge, but also on training on healing the broken hearts and setting the captives free and on developing intimacy with the Father" ....

On January 20, 1994 the Holy Spirit fell on a small church called The Toronto Airport Vineyard Christian Fellowship; and so the Toronto Blessing was born.[41] Millions of people and tens of thousands of churches around the world have been impacted by this visitation of the Holy Spirit. I can affirm that every portion of this prophesy has come true. The church has opened eight training Schools of Ministry around the world; and it has focused on the Father's love, healing and inner healing. In addition it has opened churches in sixteen cities around the world plus nine church campuses in the Greater Toronto Area. You can read more about this in the book *From Here To The Nations*,[42] and also view the church website at catchthefire.com.

---

41   This church is now called *Catch The Fire*.
42   ibid.

Prophetic Word Over a Nation:

Even as far back as the 1700's there has been prophetic words that Canada has a special place in God's plan. In the 1920's Smith Wigglesworth, the famous British Healing Evangelist, foretold of the significant revival that would break out in Saskatchewan in the late 1940's. This was fulfilled on February 12, 1948 when the Holy Spirit fell on a group of believers in North Battleford, Saskatchewan.[43] Soon people came from all across North America and from around the world to witness this new wave of the Holy Spirit.

As we saw earlier, the 1994 revival that broke out in Toronto was prophesied by Mark DuPont, and more recently prophets such as Stacy Campbell and Cindy Jacobs are proclaiming that another great outpouring is coming to Canada soon. And this outpouring of the Spirit will be much, much greater than any preceding move; and again it will spread to the ends of the world. This anticipated revival is also featured in an outstanding prophetic documentary video entitled "From the River to the Ends of the Earth" by Marney Blom.[44] This work examines Canada's spiritual identity and destiny and features First Nations and Inuit spiritual leaders whom affirm through dreams and visions their belief that Canada is moving towards an unprecedented spiritual awakening. The title is taken from the text carved in stone on Canada's Parliament building "He shall have dominion from sea to sea and from the River to the

43   Fred & Sharon Wright, The World's Greatest Revivals, Destiny Image Publishers, 2007 page 187-188.

44   From the River to the Ends of the Earth by Marney Blom, produced by Canadian Acts News Network, website actsnewsnetwork.com

ends of the earth" Psalm 72:8. You can find more information about this work, including a video clip, at the website given in the footnote below. I also recommend a book entitled *Canada Book of Decrees and Prophecies*;[45] therein you can read for yourself some of the prophetic Words spoken over the nation of Canada.

As you can see from the examples cited above, prophecy still occurs today and it works! It worked in the Old Testament, as more than three hundred prophecies concerning the Messiah came true in Jesus Christ. Personal prophecy has worked and inspired me in my journey, and corporate prophecy over Toronto and the nation of Canada has also proved true. Corporate prophecy is of course not limited to Canada, I'm just using an at-hand example. The point is, God is faithful to complete all that He says and promises; as was spoken by the prophet in Isaiah 55:10-11, above.

Let's pray:

Lord God, we thank you that you continue to speak to us today, with words of instruction, words of encouragement and sometimes words of warning.

Pour out your spirit as you did at Pentecost and give your prophets the boldness to speak forth your message, especially during these days.

Lord, give us ears to hear and eyes to see as you speak to us in dreams, visions, and prophetic words.

45   Canada Book of Decrees and Prophecies, V-Kol Media Ministries, 2014 website ears2hear.ca

Help us to discern your truth, and give us the wisdom to act on it.

We ask this prayer in Jesus name. Amen

Further Meditation

Are you actively listening to God speaking to the church today?

_____

_____

_____

_____

_____

_____

_____

_____

_____

_____

_____

_____

_____

_____

_____

_____

_____

_____

_____

Conquering Abuse
and Persecution

Then one of them, named Caiaphas, who was high priest that year, spoke
up, "You know nothing at all! You do not realize that it is better for you that
one man die for the people than that the whole nation perish." So from that
day on they plotted to take his life.

JOHN 11:49-50 & 53

"Come to me, all you who are weary and burdened, and I will give you rest.
Take my yoke upon you and learn from me, for I am gentle and humble in
heart, and you will find rest for your souls."

MATTHEW 11:28-29

Have you ever been physically or emotionally abused by others? It's a regrettable fact that many of us have. What about
that bully at school, or an abusive parent, boss or even your
spouse? It's especially cruel when the abuser is someone who is
supposed to protect and nurture us. As a spiritual counselor, I
often meet with people suffering from addictions or emotional
problems; frequently the root cause of their trouble is physical
or emotional abuse during childhood.

Here is a true story about betrayal and redemption. On this
occasion, I was asked to act as chaperone to a group of young
adults going to a conference in Steubenville, Ohio. During a
healing service, one of the girls in our group started to laugh

uncontrollably, and there was nothing we could do to stop her. After some time we had to call for medical assistance as she was becoming visibly distressed and unable to breathe properly. Finally, she calmed down and recovered.

On the full-day bus ride home, we invited the young people to share their testimonies of the weekend. This young girl took the microphone and told us her story about her laughing experience. She was from a poor village in Asia and when she was about twelve years old she was sexually assaulted by her uncle. When she told her parents they looked away in sadness and said "You must permit this for the family, we need the money". So the assaults continued, not only from her uncle, but from other men in the village too.

She went on to explain that during the healing service Jesus came to her and together they went back to this episode in her life. And as Jesus broke the chains of guilt and shame from her, they both started to laugh at the demons of lust that had been on her abusers.[46] She experienced the "joy of the Lord"[47] as never before and now knew her true identity in Christ, as His beloved daughter.

Another form of abuse is being falsely accused by others. If you have experienced this, then you have something in common with Jesus. He was betrayed by a close friend, taken to a place of false judgment in front of religious leaders, wrongfully

---

46   Psalm 37:13 ... but the Lord laughs at the wicked, for he knows their day is coming.

47   Romans 14:17 For the kingdom of God is not a matter of eating and drinking, but of righteousness, peace and joy in the Holy Spirit, Galatians 5:22-23 But the fruit of the Spirit is love, joy, peace, forbearance, kindness, goodness, faithfulness, gentleness and self-control. Against such things there is no law.

accused by lying witnesses, brutally tortured and finally put to death. During His ordeal he asked His Father if he could escape from this fate, but he also added "not my will but your will be done."

> *Going a little farther, he fell with his face to the ground and prayed, "My Father, if it is possible, may this cup be taken from me. Yet not as I will, but as you will."*
>
> MATTHEW 26:39

I was once also falsely accused by a group of my peers in a church situation, so I know something of the emotional pain that Jesus went through. But I have to confess that I did not act with the same grace that Jesus displayed. I would gladly have seen my accusers suffer the humiliation and pain that I was going through, but it did not work out that way at all. As I cried out to God for justice, I believe that I received the following word from the Holy Spirit, which over time, took away my fears and allowed me to endure and forgive those who falsely accused me. I still re-read this word today when I am facing difficult and troublesome circumstances.

After you receive a word from the Holy Spirit it's good practice to search for biblical references, in order to confirm the source of the word. I have included these references for the word, below.

So if you are troubled for any reason, I invite you to allow these words to reach deeply into your heart—they come from the Heart of God.

Swim Deep

Swim deep, my child ... go deep[48] As a fish swims in the water, so swim in me.[49] Breath in me, be absorbed in me... abide in my presence.[50] Drink of my Holy Spirit[51]...

I am controlling the storms that you see raging all around you,[52] Swim deep and you will find calm water where the storm cannot reach.

Trust me. Seek my wisdom in all the events of your life My ways are not your ways, my thought are not your thoughts.[53] Do not rely on your human wisdom Rely on me and trust my ways[54]

I am your Father,[55] I love you and want the very best for you, And I have a perfect plan and destiny for you. Pray that this plan will unfold before you and that you will follow my ways[56] Then, I can bless you as I want to bless you.[57]

I love you my child, Come rest in my arms, I love you.

---

48   Psalm 42:7
49   Ezekiel 47:1-47
50   John 15:1-10
51   John 4:13-14
52   Matthew 14:22-33
53   Isaiah 55:8
54   2 Corinthians 1:12
55   Romans 5:18, Galatians 4:6
56   Psalm 40:5 & Jeremiah 29:11
57   Deuteronomy 28:1-14

Further Meditation

Do you believe that God has a perfect plan for you? Are you willing to trust Him to work it out?

_____

_____

_____

_____

_____

_____

_____

_____

_____

_____

Take your own troubles to Jesus and ask Him to speak words to you about them—journal His response.

_____

_____

_____

_____

_____

_____

_____

_____

_____

_____

The God of Fire

When all the Israelites saw the fire coming down and the glory of the LORD above the temple, they knelt on the pavement with their faces to the ground, and they worshiped and gave thanks to the LORD, saying, "He is good; his love endures forever."

2 CHRONICLES 7:3

But who can endure the day of his coming? Who can stand when he appears? For he will be like a refiner's fire or a launderer's soap. He will sit as a refiner and purifier of silver; he will purify the Levites and refine them like gold and silver. Then the LORD will have men who will bring offerings in righteousness.

MALACHI 3:2-3

In both the scriptures above, God appears as fire. In the first, the fire of God causes his people to bow down in awe and to worship Him as a good and loving God. In the second, the prophet Malachi speaks of the fire of God as a refining or purifying fire. These two images of God seem very different don't they? The image of God as launderer's soap is particularly vivid for me, as it takes me back to my childhood during World War II, and being scrubbed in the bath tub with harsh yellow laundry soap. Ugh!

As I meditated on these scriptures as an adult I realized that sometimes we have to destroy the old before we enable the new. A good example of this would be a forest fire, which is nature's way of destroying the old wood to allow and enrich new growth. In the refiner's oven ore is heated until the precious metals are released in their molten form. In this way, the metallurgist separates the pure metal from the dross. This seems to be exactly what Malachi is referring to.

The Holy Spirit is also referred to as the fire of God and of course, this is how He appeared on the day of Pentecost. It's interesting that John the Baptist also refers to the refining nature of this Holy Fire. *"I baptize you with water for repentance. But after me comes one who is more powerful than I, whose sandals I am not worthy to carry. He will baptize you with the Holy Spirit and fire. His winnowing fork is in his hand, and he will clear his threshing floor, gathering his wheat into the barn and burning up the chaff with unquenchable fire" (Matthew 3:11-12).*

Should we be afraid of the Fire of God? In my experience we should respect it but not fear it. Below, I include two of my journal entries from January 2010. These occurred during one of those "mountain top" experiences where I was blessed with the intense burning presence of God, for several nights in a row. Oh that we could stay with Him on the mountaintop, but it doesn't work that way, does it? Even Moses had to come down from the mountaintop, and what did he find? In only 40 days, his people had forgotten their God, and were back worshipping golden idols.

Here is my journal entry… "In one encounter with the Lord I felt a large fireball, about the size of an orange or baseball. It landed in my heart and later moved down into the top part of my stomach (my gut). It was intensely hot, about all I could bear, yet at the same time it felt good and I didn't want it to stop. I asked the Lord what was happening and He said, "This is my refiner's fire; it is my truth and it will set you free and transform you". And then I recalled Jesus' words *"Whoever believes in me, as Scripture has said, out of his belly will flow rivers of living water, by this he meant the Spirit, whom those who believed in him were later to receive" (John 7:38-39).*

During this time, I also received this word ...

The Fire of My Love

My Child, I love you with a fiery love,[58] *A love that burns as hot as the sun.*

I loved you into existence at the beginning of time, And I hold you in that love today.[59]

A passionate love. A holy love. A perfect love. A love that will never fail.[60] *A love that will never diminish or grow cold.*

My child, draw close to me,[61] *Reach into the depth of my love. Swim in the golden river that is my love for you.*[62]

My child, trust me always. Never doubt that my love is with you My love endures forever.

---

58   2 Chronicles 7:3 Song of Songs 8:6
59   Deuteronomy 33:3
60   Exodus 15:13 Psalm 138:2
61   James 4:8
62   Ezekiel 47:1-47

A Father's love My love.[63]

Yes my child, I am your Father, and I love you with a father's love.[64]

Peace be with you,[65] *I am with you, always.*[66]

Further Meditation

Can you recall times when God was working to refine or purify you?

_____

_____

_____

_____

_____

_____

How has this affected your life?

_____

_____

_____

_____

_____

_____

63   1 John 4:8, 12 John 4:16
64   1 John 3
65   Luke 24:36 John 14:27, 20:19, 20:21, 20:26
66   Matthew 28:20

On Eagles' Wings

Then Moses went up to God, and the LORD called to him from the mountain and said, "This is what you are to say to the descendants of Jacob and what you are to tell the people of Israel: 'You yourselves have seen what I did to Egypt, and how I carried you on eagles' wings and brought you to myself.'"

EXODUS 19:3-4

The LORD is the everlasting God, the Creator of the ends of the earth. He will not grow tired or weary, and his understanding no one can fathom. He gives strength to the weary and increases the power of the weak. Even youths grow tired and weary, and young men stumble and fall; but those who hope in the LORD will renew their strength. They will soar on wings like eagles; they will run and not grow weary, they will walk and not be faint.

ISAIAH 40:28-31

I think we can learn a lot from the eagle; surely the most graceful yet powerful of all birds. Did you know they mate for life, raise their offspring together, and protect them from the harsh weather in the shelter of their wings? They build their nests in the tops of tall trees or high up on craggy cliffs, and when it's time to teach their young to fly, the mother eagle pushes them out of the nest into the air, and the father eagle flying below catches them on his back and brings them safely back to the nest.

Eagles are designed for power. They are the only birds that

love storms. While other birds seek safety from the storm, eagles will fly directly into it, using the pressure of the storm to soar higher and higher. And on calmer days they use these same powerful wings to glide gracefully on the air currents, as they employ their extraordinary eyesight to seek out food. Eagles have exceptional eyesight, estimated to be 4 to 8 times stronger than human eyesight. They see in colour and can easily distinguish between different coloured prey; it is said that they can spot a rabbit 2 miles away. As the eagle descends from the sky to attack its prey, at speeds well over 100 miles per hour, the muscles in their eyes continuously adjust in order to maintain sharp focus for the attack. Their eyesight also adapts to refraction so that they can catch fish swimming below the surface of water.

The Hebrew writers of the Old Testament must have spent hours looking into the sky and marveling at the eagle's exceptional gifts. And as they did, they related this to their image of God; here are further examples:

Look! He advances like the clouds, his chariots come like a whirlwind, his horses are swifter than eagles.

JEREMIAH 4:13

Does the eagle mount up at your command, and make its nest on high? On the rock it dwells and resides, on the crag of the rock and the stronghold. From there it spies out the prey; its eyes observe from afar.

JOB 39:27-29

Our pursuers were swifter than eagles in the sky.

LAMENTATIONS 4:19

With all this in mind, I was prompted to write this prayer below, which is adapted from Michael Joncas' popular song *On Eagles Wings*, Psalm 91 and Isaiah 40:31.

On Eagle's Wings[67]

He will raise you up on Eagle's wings, bear you on the breath of dawn, make you shine like the sun, and hold you in the palm of His hand.

You need not fear the terrors of the night, nor the arrows that fly by day, nor the enemy that stalks in the darkness, nor the plague that ravages at noon.

They that hope in the Lord will renew their strength, they will soar as with eagles' wings; they will run and not grow weary, walk and never tire.

Though a thousand fall at your side, ten thousand at your right hand, you yourself will remain unharmed, for you have placed your trust in the Lord.

I rescue all who seek me, I protect whoever knows My name, I answer every one who calls to me, I am with them when they are in trouble. I bring them safety and honor, with long (eternal) life I will bless them, and show them my saving power.

---

67 Adapted from Psalm 91, Isaiah 40:31 and the hymn "On Eagle's Wings" by Michael Joncas.

Further Meditation

Allow The Holy Spirit to guide you as you write you own prayer based on God revealing Himself in nature.

_____

_____

_____

_____

_____

_____

_____

_____

_____

_____

_____

_____

_____

_____

_____

_____

_____

_____

_____

_____

_____

_____

_____

_____

Walking in Expectant Faith

Now faith is confidence in what we hope for and assurance about what we do not see.

HEBREWS 11:1

It was by faith that Noah built an ark to save his family.
It was by faith that Abraham obeyed the call to set out from a country without knowing where he was going.
It was by faith that Sarah, in spite of being passed the age, was made able to conceive.
It was by faith that Abraham, when put to the test, offered up his son Isaac.
It was by faith that Moses was hidden by his parents.
It was through faith that the walls of Jericho fell down when the people marched around them for seven days.

EXTRACTED FROM HEBREWS 11:7-31

You may be thinking "what's the difference between 'regular' faith and 'expectant' faith?" Well it has to do with the level, or strength, of that faith. We see from Hebrews 11:1 that faith is having a sure confidence in someone or something unseen. But in the face of extreme difficulty, how strong is our confidence, how strong is our faith?

Have you ever tried bungee jumping off a bridge or cliff with only the bungee rope keeping you from almost certain death? What about skydiving from an airplane? Would you do that?

My sons, Rich and Rob, have done both between them, and I'm glad that they didn't tell me about it before they jumped. I don't think that I could muster up the faith, or the courage to do either of these stunts. Isn't it interesting that faith and courage go together when we are testing our limits? Sometimes God asks us for this level of faith in Him, and that is called expectant faith.

The stories of Noah, Abraham, Sarah, the mother of Moses and the Israelites at Jericho, as described in the scripture above, are examples of extraordinary faith. These people were likely considered crazy by their friends and neighbours, yet all of them stepped out with faith and courage in God. They heard from the Lord and they acted despite what their friends and neighbours thought and said.

In the Healing Rooms training workshops we learn that faith has to be acted upon to produce results. In other words, it's not enough to believe or hope that a supernatural healing will take place. We have to do something about it and step out in faith. When we know God's will and exercise the authority that he has given us, then miracles happen.

Steve Long tells an amazing story of how expectant faith produces miracles in his book *My Healing Belongs to Me.*[68] In this story, a Nigerian Pastor had died and was already embalmed with formaldehyde in preparation for the funeral. Reinhard Bonnke, a famous Healing Evangelist, was in town and the man's wife decided to take his body to the service, trusting for a miracle. When she got to the church she was not allowed to take the body into the service, so she took him to

68   Steve Long, My Healing Belongs to Me, Catch The Fire Books, 2014, page 79.

the basement instead and placed the body on a table. One of the assistant pastors heard her story and joined her downstairs and they began to pray in faith for a resurrection miracle, despite the fact that the body had been embalmed and contained no blood. Sometime later the body began to breathe, move and eventually the man rose up—alive. This miracle was captured on videotape and verified by several reliable sources, including Reinhard Bonnke. The man, who apparently smelt of formaldehyde for months, made a complete recovery and went on to father two more children. Now that's supernatural!

None of us is born with expectant faith. It comes as a gift from the Holy Spirit, but fortunately we can strengthen and nourish our faith through prayer and spiritual exercises. When I need to boost my faith levels I often read Hebrews chapter 11, which reminds me how many times God supported the Israelites in their difficulties. I also try to think of the many times He has supported me. For example, sometimes I intentionally recall the dream I had about stepping out onto the unfinished bridge over the Grand Canyon (see Day 14), or I remind myself of the many healing miracles that I have seen.

Let's pray for expectant faith:

Lord, increase my faith to believe in miracles. And to believe that the miracles described in the Bible, are still available for me, today.

Help me to hear what you are saying to me, and to act on your word, with faith and courage.

Help me to shut out all the talk of the enemy, and even my friends, who would try to discourage me. Help me persevere in the face of discouragement. Keep doubt and unbelief from me.

Lord God, give me expectant faith, like you gave Noah, Abraham and Moses, then, help me to focus on you and the desires of your heart. Since you are for me I will overcome all adversity. Jesus I trust you, let your will prevail in my life... Amen

Further Meditation

Think of a time when you acted (stepped out) in faith.

_____

_____

_____

_____

_____

_____

_____

What did you learn from this? Are you ready to do it again?

_____

_____

_____

_____

_____

_____

_____

Speaking in Tongues

All of them were filled with the Holy Spirit, and began to speak in other tongues, as the Spirit enabled them.

ACTS 2:4

Now to each one the manifestation of the Spirit is given for the common good. To one there is given through the Spirit a message of wisdom, to another a message of knowledge by means of the same Spirit, to another faith by the same Spirit, to another gifts of healing by that one Spirit, to another miraculous powers, to another prophecy, to another distinguishing between spirits, to another speaking in different kinds of tongues, and to still another the interpretation of tongues. All these are the work of one and the same Spirit, and he distributes them to each one, just as he determines.

1 CORINTHIANS 12:7-11

Millions of people around the world and in many denominations have received the gift of speaking in tongues. It is, in fact, one of the defining characteristics of the Pentecostal/ Charismatic renewal.[69] To those that have received this gift it is a wonderful and uplifting experience. To those who have not experienced it, it is often a mystifying and divisive issue. Yet it is one of the spiritual gifts spoken of in the scripture above, so let's explore it further.

There are different forms of speaking in tongues. One is

---

69 For more detail of Charismatic Renewal see Fred & Sharon Wright, The World's Greatest Revivals, Destiny Image Publishing, 2007.

a public gift, mentioned above and is used in community to encourage and inspire those present. I witnessed this gift several years ago at a church conference, when an English speaking man starting prophesying in Japanese, yet this man had never studied Japanese and could not speak the language. Even he needed interpretation of what he was saying himself. Why God did this, I don't know; but it certainly amazed and encouraged those who witnessed it.

Another form of tongue is the personal gift, and it is used for private prayer. I sometimes find myself spontaneously praying in tongues during my prayer time or when I am listening to worship music. It seems to come bubbling up from somewhere inside of me. It's not an understandable human language and is sometimes referred to as the praise language of angels or even the prayer language of the Holy Spirit. It can be considered as a form of contemplative prayer as it allows me to disconnect my mind and voice from my physical surroundings and to enter into the realm of the spirit. It's a spiritual language and as with many things of the spirit, it is difficult to rationalize.

In the healing ministry, I sometimes pray in tongues especially when I am trying to determine what the Lord wants to do for the person receiving prayer. In this ministry, we are taught to listen to the requestor with one ear and to God with the other. It is amazing how frequently two prayer ministers will receive the same prompting of what the Lord wants to bring about, and it can be quite different from what the person originally wanted. For instance, a person requesting prayer is likely focused on their current condition, but the Lord may first wish to heal something in their past; this occurred to the lady I had a word of knowledge for, described in Day 21. Knowing God's will allows us to bring His perfect healing solution into a person's life.

Sometimes during prayer ministry I run out of words to say, and then just enter into tongues. It's a lot better than repeating myself, or even worse, bargaining with God. After all, the Father already knows what we will ask for, and what He plans to do.[70]

On one occasion I was praying with a young man suffering from severe depression. He had been too depressed to leave the house for some time and finally his wife "persuaded" (dragged) him into the prayer-room. He admitted that he had fried his brain on psychedelic drugs and couldn't think straight; he was in a desperate situation. As I laid hands on him and prayed in tongues, I knew that God was touching him so I just continued in tongues and let God do His work. After five or six minutes of praying he was a different person and described how he felt as if something was burning away all the wrong connections in his brain and re-wiring good connections. He was healed and went back to work shortly afterwards. Praise God!

I wrote earlier that the gift of tongues is sometimes described as the praise language of angels. Let me share this experience with you. It occurred when I was attending a conference at my church. At the end of an awesome praise and worship session, the congregation spontaneously began to sing in tongues. There were more than one thousand people

---

70   Psalm 139:4

present, from all over the world. All the voices and tongues blended together perfectly as the sound moved around the room and the volume rose and fell, all in a perfect symphony. At one point it sounded like a strong wind and I knew in my spirit that this is what scripture described at Pentecost. *"And suddenly there came a sound from heaven, as of a rushing mighty wind, and it filled the whole house where they were sitting"*.[71] I'm convinced that the "powerful wind from Heaven" was actually a heavenly host of angels, singing praises to God, in their heavenly language.

As we have seen in scripture, the gift of tongues is a special gift from the Holy Spirit and is intended to be used to encourage, heal and strengthen His people. It comes most frequently as part of the download or Baptism in the Holy Spirit described in Day 15. Sometimes a person may just receive the gift spontaneously, as I did. I even heard a lady say that she received her gift of tongues as she was washing dishes at the kitchen sink. So we don't have to understand everything with our minds. Just let go, and let God!

If you would like to experience the gift of tongues, talk to a friend who has this gift, or your pastor, your prayer group or prayer ministry team and ask them to pray with you for the Baptism in the Spirit and the gift of tongues. As mentioned earlier, different churches and denominations have varying ways to impart this gift; hopefully they will give you further teaching on this subject and then pray with you. If your church does not encourage this revelation, you may have to search

71 Acts 2:2

outside your local community. As mentioned in Day 15, the charismatic gifts are intended for use within a church community, so pray about this carefully before you take action.

The prayer below is intended for those who wish to experience this gift. Ideally, it is advisable that you have people to support you as you mature in the use of this gift.

When speaking in tongues, it is necessary to yield your vocal chords to the moving of the Holy Spirit. You are choosing to speak but choosing not to control the formation of the words that flow out of your mouth. You are also choosing to believe that what flows out is under the control of the Holy Spirit. Initially it's helpful to start repeating, out loud and over and over again, a single word like alleluia … alleluia … alleluia, or a single syllable like ba… ba… ba, until your new prayer language just comes bubbling out.

Holy Spirit, I come before you with the desire to praise you in your heavenly language.

Loosen my vocal chords to resonate to your frequency and release me to worship you in spirit and in truth. I ask for the gift of speaking in tongues, as promised in scripture.

Come Holy Spirit, come. I receive your gift by faith.

Don't become discouraged if this does not seem to work the first time, keep trying. But, after trying prayerfully for some time, perhaps you should consult with someone you trust and who knows your spiritual walk. The Lord will reward your persistence. Remember this is a gift from God so we need to do it His way, and it is better to be in community with like minded people, than to try going it alone.

Further Meditation

If you have received the gift of tongues how would you help others to receive it?

_____

_____

_____

_____

_____

_____

_____

If you have not yet received it, ask someone you know who has this gift to pray with you.

_____

_____

_____

_____

_____

_____

_____

Dreaming God-Dreams

Pharaoh said to Joseph, "I had a dream, and no one can interpret it. But I have heard it said of you that when you hear a dream you can interpret it." "I cannot do it," Joseph replied to Pharaoh, "but God will give Pharaoh the answer he desires."

GENESIS 41:15-15

I will pour out my spirit on all mankind, your sons and daughters shall prophesy your old men shall dream dreams.

JOEL 3:1 AND ACTS 2:17

I don't personally consider myself to be an old man yet (though you might), but the Lord has started to speak to me in dreams. Maybe it's because He likes to wait until I'm asleep to reach into my more intuitive side. Being left-brained, I tend to keep my intuitive and expressive side under lock and key during the day. But in dreams we go into a more right brained realm, where the laws of gravity no longer apply, and time and space have no logical order. Definitely not my world! Yet here, in dreams, I have learned that God does speak to me.

In his book *Hear God through your Dreams*,[72] Mark Virkler gives practical guidelines for understanding and

---

72   Hear God Through Your Dreams, by Mark & Patty Virkler, 2011, available at Christian bookstores or from cwgministries.org

interpreting your dreams. Here are some key guidelines to
get you started:

» Believe that God does indeed speak to you in your
   dreams.[73]
» Write them down as soon as you wake up.
» As you re-read the dream, ask the Holy Spirit to help
   you understand the spiritual message in the dream.
   You need Holy Spirit revelation, not leaning on your
   own understanding.[74]
» If you are the main character in the dream, then this
   dream is likely about you and it will probably relate
   to a current event in your life.
» Dreams mostly come from the heart so ask yourself
   "What was I feeling in the dream?" Was it fear, frus-
   tration, excitement, contentment, etc.? "How does
   this relate to how I was recently feeling?"
» Look at the action of the dream and try to see any
   symbolism. Were you moving upwards, around in
   circles, were you falling, soaring like a bird or perhaps being hunted? Ask yourself "How does this
   relate to a current situation in my life?"
» Was there someone else in the dream? This person
   likely represents a part of your character, so what is
   this person like—analytical? Free-spirited? Angry?
   Ask yourself "Do I sometimes behave like this?"
   Dreams are symbolic and highly personalized.

73   Numbers 12:6; Job 33:14-16; Daniel 1:17; Acts 16:9; Matthew 1:20, 2:13, 2:19
74   I Corinthians 2:10, Proverbs 3:5

So ask yourself, "What does this symbol mean to me?" A house, for instance, could signify safety or danger; a work situation could represent success or failure.

» God may be speaking to you for your instruction, and if so, you are being called to act upon your dreams. But please show caution in all of this and remember that dreams are highly symbolic. If you have a dream that takes place in a far off country, it does not necessarily mean you are supposed to sell your home and move there. Ask yourself "What does this country signify to me?"

» Finally, when in doubt about the interpretation of your dream, seek help from a trusted friend, and pray for confirmation from the Lord.

Here are two examples from my dream-life; I trust you will see how the guidelines above can be applied to their interpretation.

In one dream, I was sitting on a school bus with a group of friends; we were driving through a busy city. Later, I found myself driving the bus, and it was fun negotiating my way through all the traffic. We came to a stop sign, and I stopped and put on the handbrake, but the bus started to roll backwards and there was nothing I could do to stop it. Then there was a sickening crunch, and I realized I had backed into a cyclist, and knocked him to the ground. As I got off the bus to see what had happened I met two burly policemen, notebooks in hand. I was arrested for dangerous driving.

At this point I awoke, still a little scared, and asked God, "Lord, that was not a very nice dream, what does it mean?" In a flash I heard the words "Look who was driving the bus". Then I knew exactly what the dream was all about.

You see, that evening I had experienced a difficult meeting with the leadership team of our healing school. I felt I was not getting the support I needed from them, and we were sliding backwards in certain areas. In the dream the Lord was saying to me, "Stop driving the bus. Give up some of your controlling ways. This is my healing school, not yours." As I obeyed this instruction, the healing school went from strength to strength, and I learned a valuable lesson in giving control to the Lord.

In another dream, two friends and I were in England, trying to find someone; I don't know who. I was a child at the time and became separated from my friends; I was lost and felt scared. I wandered around in the City of Oxford, alone and afraid. Eventually, I came to a tourist office where a loving, friendly lady gave me a map and helped me find my way home. When I awoke I felt anxious and a bit scared. I asked the Lord, "What was that all about, Lord?"

Immediately I heard the words: "Now you know something about how (name) feels." I knew this related to a friend who was suffering from anxiety and depression at the time. The Lord allowed me to experience a little of his pain, so that I could become more compassionate and understanding towards him. He also showed me that I needed to exercise more love and compassion in order to help him find the way home. I'm pleased to say that it worked: from that moment forward, I found I had much more patience when relating to him. I learned that pushing him to do things my way was not going to help. He needed love and support, not heavy-handed direction.

For further reading on the purpose and interpretation of dreams, I recommend *Dream Dreams*[75] and also *Dreams that Heal and Counsel*[76] by Steve and Dianne Bydeley.

Let's pray for hearing God speak to us in dreams and prophesies:

Lord, let me hear your voice. I give you permission Lord, to speak to me in prophecy and in dreams. Lord, you know my every need, I welcome your healing word into my life. During sleep, I open my spirit to your Holy Spirit and my mind to your thoughts.

By your grace, I promise to act Lord, as you direct. I pray that you would grant me the gift of interpreting my dreams. To bring your mercy and love to my brothers and sisters.

Speak Lord your servant is listening.

I ask this prayer in Jesus' name. Amen.

75 Steve and Dianne Bydeley, Dream Dreams., Essence Publishing, 2002.
76 Steve and Dianne Bydeley, Dreams that heal and Counsel, Lapstone Ministries, 2004.

Further Meditation

Has God ever spoken to you in a dream? Write it down and seek its interpretation. Then seek confirmation from other like-minded Christians.

_____

_____

_____

_____

_____

_____

_____

_____

_____

If you are not aware if God has ever spoken to you in a dream, why do you think that is?

_____

_____

_____

_____

_____

_____

_____

_____

_____

Discovering God's Plan
for Your Life

"For I know the plans I have for you," declares the LORD, "plans to prosper you and not to harm you, plans to give you hope and a future."

JEREMIAH 29:11

But the plans of the LORD stand firm forever, the purposes of his heart through all generations.

PSALM 33:11

Wow, these scriptures say that God has a plan and purpose for my life. This thought didn't occur to me as I was growing up; in fact I didn't think much about it for a good part of my adult life too. What about you?

It reminds me of the famous Footsteps[77] prayer that my wife and I have hanging on our kitchen wall. You've likely heard the story, how a man is walking on a beach with the Lord and looking back over his life as a series of footsteps in the sand. He sees that during the really difficult times in his life there is only one set of footprints. Thinking that he was alone, even abandoned during these times, he asks the Lord about this, and the Lord responds "Where there is only one set of footprints they are mine, that was when I was carrying

---

77   You can find the full story at footstepsinthesand.com

you." This is a beautiful story, and points to the truth that God is a loving God and does care for us, in the good times and the bad. God does have a plan for your life, and he does carry you through all your difficult days.

I love the story of Joseph in the Old Testament;[78] in fact, he is one of my heroes. The story is simple: Joseph receives two God-dreams, which unfortunately he does not handle well, and this causes problems between him and his brothers. Out of envy they throw him into a deep well, fake his death and sell him into slavery where he is falsely accused of adultery. He ends up in Pharaoh's jail, where he remains for 13 years. Eventually, God gives Joseph the ability to interpret Pharaoh's dreams, and as a result Joseph is appointed Chief Executive Officer (or Prime Minister) over all Egypt in a time of great famine. He is eventually reconciled with his brothers and reunited with his father, and continues to live a long and prosperous life.

I know it seems like a fairy tale, doesn't it? But God's thumbprint is all over this story. Through all the ups and downs of Joseph's life, God's protection and provision was on him: Joseph was a man who knew and trusted God, regardless of circumstances. I don't suppose he always understood what was going on, and may have questioned God at times. But, it is evident that he was a man of character who persevered in doing right in the face of sometimes overwhelming circumstances. And he was rewarded with the administration of great wealth and responsibility, a restored relationship with

78   Genesis chapters 37 to 50.

his family, and with a place in history. Through his actions, the Jewish nation was saved from starvation, prospered, and multiplied to fill the entire region.

So what do I learn from this story? First, it is a God-story, not a fairy tale and the message is in complete agreement with the scripture quoted at the beginning of this reading. God was present with Joseph and had a plan for him even when he was betrayed by his brothers, thrown into the well, and later, when he was cast into prison. God also used these events for His purposes and so positioned Joseph, and his sometimes treacherous brothers, to become founders of the twelve tribes of Israel.

As I look back on my life I can see that God has a plan for me. However I have to admit that I have not always seen or acknowledged it. I now recognize His steady hand guiding me throughout my entire life. In my birth family, surviving World War II; my Catholic upbringing; moving to Canada and marrying my wife, Marion. I see Him in my family, career, and especially in His download of the Holy Spirit and ensuing spiritual gifts. I see Him leading me to join my current church and into the healing and counseling ministries.

So what about you? As you think back on your life can you see God's hand guiding you? As you went through hard times, was he supporting you? If you wandered away for a while, can you see Him calling you back? Maybe His help came in the form of a helpful friend, or a lucky break, and you didn't recognize it at the time.

I realize that we are not all called to be "Josephs", but I do believe that God has a plan and purpose for each one of us. It's as if He is building a giant jigsaw puzzle, or a mosaic, with billions and billions of pieces. And each one of us is an individual piece, each with our own colour, texture and position in His work of art. Our job is to agree and cooperate with Him, "the master-craftsman."

If you are not aware of God's purpose for your life, there are several ways you can discover His plan. I recommend Rick Warren's devotional book *The Purpose Driven Life*,[79] which has sold more than 30 million copies and is claimed to be the second most translated book after the Bible. Another book that I found extremely helpful is called *Dream Culture*.[80] This book taught me how to discover my destiny and offered concrete steps to prepare a plan plus coaching to bring my plan into action. Another good resource is Lance Wallnau's website, which is full of useful learning aids. I found his "21 Questions That Will Change Your Life",[81] particularly helpful.

Let's pray that you will have revelation of God's plan for your life:

Father I come to you seeking your plan and purpose for my life. I admit that I have mostly pursued my own plans, but now Lord I would like to discover what your plan is for me.

Lord, I give you my life. And I trust you to help me find your plan and purpose.

79   Rick Warren, Purpose Driven Life, Zondervan Books, 2012.
80   Andy and Janine Mason, Dream Culture, 2011 can be purchased at Christian
      bookstores of from idreamculture.com
81   Downloaded from lanacelearning.com

Lord, I have a special situation that I am dealing with right now, (name it) and I give you this situation now.

Lord, I can't solve this alone, I truly need to know your will and to have your help.

Lord, still my mind and my thoughts so that I can hear you speak to me. I ask for your wisdom and understanding. Send your ministering angels to support me in my struggles. And where necessary, send your servants to help me with this situation. Then encourage me to do what is right, in your eyes.

And as I continue on my life's journey, I ask for your continued presence and favour. Help me to discern your plans and purposes for my life. Open those doors that I need to be opened and shut the doors that I don't need to go through.

Keep me close to you, each day for the rest of my life.

I ask this in Jesus name. Amen.

Further Meditation

Do you know God's plan for your life?

_____

_____

_____

_____

_____

_____

_____

_____

_____

If it's not written down, then write it down now. If it is, then perhaps re-read it and update it.

_____

_____

_____

_____

_____

_____

_____

_____

If you don't know God's plan for your life, please check out my recommendations above (or other material) and prayerfully get to work!

_____

_____

_____

_____

_____

_____

_____

_____

A Call to Service

"Teacher, which is the greatest commandment in the Law?" Jesus replied: "'Love the Lord your God with all your heart and with all your soul and with all your mind.' This is the first and greatest commandment. And the second is like it: 'Love your neighbor as yourself.' All the Law and the Prophets hang on these two commandments."

MATTHEW 22:36-40

Then Jesus came to them and said, "All authority in heaven and on earth has been given to me. Therefore go and make disciples of all nations, baptizing them in the name of the Father and of the Son and of the Holy Spirit, and teaching them to obey everything I have commanded you. And surely I am with you always, to the very end of the age."

MATTHEW 28:18-20

In my experience, being called into God's service and having a God-plan for my life is pretty much the same thing. Two sides of the same coin, if you will.

I'm not really sure when my first call came. Was it at my baptism, my confirmation, at my first Cursillo weekend, or my spirit filled baptism? Or was it one continuous call from God, as He watched over me throughout my whole life? I'm really not sure.

Regardless of when it happened, the vision described below was one of the greatest signs or messages from the Holy Spirit that I have ever received. It transformed my life—I have never been the same since. Let it speak to you.

God's Love, Poured Out

In my spirit, I saw a shiny metal bucket, a milking pail specifically. Then the pail was being filled with a thick, warm, golden liquid, just like honey. It was filled to the very top, until it could hold no more. I understood this to be God pouring His love into my entire being.[82] I was totally at peace, and thanked Him for His grace and mercy.

Suddenly, the pail started to leak and a small stream of the golden liquid poured out. Then another leak, then another, until there were many golden streams pouring out from the pail. I became concerned and asked God what was happening. What had I done wrong?

He smiled and said "Don't worry my child, you haven't done anything wrong. These golden streams are streams of my grace, flowing out from you onto your troubled world.[83] You don't understand yet, but I want you (and all My people) to be a source of my grace and goodness to the world. That is why I filled you with My grace in the first place". "Oh Lord, that's okay then," I seemed to say.

As I watched, more holes were punched in the pail, and more grace poured out. I had a sense of pain and ask the Lord, "Does it hurt when you punch holes in my pail?" Immediately, I was taken in my spirit to the cross of Calvary and I saw the Roman soldiers nailing Jesus to the cross. But these weren't

82 Romans 5:5
83 John 7:38

ordinary nails; they were spikes about twelve inches long and almost an inch in diameter. Without a word being spoken I had my answer; an authentic Christian life is not without suffering.[84]

Then I saw the pail again. This time filled with so many holes that it appeared more like a very large showerhead; and the golden liquid was pouring freely. As I watched, many more holes appeared and the pail took on the appearance of a metal sieve. It was impossible to fill the sieve.

"Lord, will the liquid ever run out?" I seemed to say. He replied, "No my child, my grace for you, and for the world, is greater than the waters flowing over Niagara Falls, it can never run out, never run dry. Haven't I said my grace is sufficient for you?[85] I will never grow weary of pouring my grace on the world."

"What I need my child is willing vessels[86], willing pails. Will you be my vessel, my child? Will you be my pail?"

84   Luke 9:23; Galatians 2:20, 5:24
85   2 Corinthians 12:9
86   Romans 9:21-23

Further Meditation

What is this message saying to you?

Write your own response to God.

Persevering with God's Plan

And I answered the king, "If it pleases the king and if your servant has found favor in his sight, let him send me to the city in Judah where my ancestors are buried so that I can rebuild it."

NEHEMIAH 2:5

From that day on, half of my men did the work, while the other half were equipped with spears, shields, bows and armor. The officers posted themselves behind all the people of Judah who were building the wall. Those who carried materials did their work with one hand and held a weapon in the other, and each of the builders wore his sword at his side as he worked.

NEHEMIAH 4:16-18

So the wall was completed on the twenty-fifth of Elul, in fifty-two days. When all our enemies heard about this, all the surrounding nations were afraid and lost their self-confidence, because they realized that this work had been done with the help of our God.

NEHEMIAH 6:15-16

Another of my Old Testament heroes is Nehemiah because he tackled an almost impossible task, against incredible opposition, and succeeded in only 52 days. I encourage you to read the whole story for yourself in Nehemiah, chapters 1 to 6. Below I will summarize the main points and add my thoughts, as we go.

The story takes place around 450 BC during the Babylonian exile. Nehemiah was the cup-bearer (wine taster) to King Artaxerxes. He was in fact a slave to the king and it was his job to taste the King's wine and to make sure it was not poisoned— a high-risk occupation! Nehemiah was a man of God and when he heard of the desperate plight of his people in Jerusalem, he fasted and prayed and then he asked the king for permission to take a leave of absence in order to go to and rebuild Jerusalem's city walls. In addition, he asked for letters of safe passage and for letters to the keepers of the king's forest to supply timber for reconstruction of the city gates. He received everything he asked for.[87]

To me, Nehemiah's request seems incredibly bold. But then I realized that he understood that this was God's plan for him, and therefore, he had the faith and courage to "just to go for it." And because God was in it all, everything worked out well for him… at first.

When he reached Jerusalem he spoke to the leaders and when they saw God's favour on the work, they agreed to start rebuilding the city walls. And this is when the persecution started. The local (non-Jewish) people started to ridicule them and accused them of plotting against the king. Nehemiah rebuked them and proclaimed "the God of heaven will give us success", and then he started to build.[88] This attitude is the same attitude that David demonstrated when he confronted Goliath.

There are still times when I hesitate and lack the courage to move forward to accomplish difficult tasks, especially when

87 Nehemiah 2:1-8
88 Nehemiah 2:17-20

I meet opposition from others. When this occurs, I find it so easy to give up. That is when my thoughts turn to Nehemiah and how he pushed forward despite the very real and sometimes life-threatening opposition. While you and I are not called to rebuild the walls of Jerusalem, I believe that God is calling us to have a similar level of faith to complete the tasks He has assigned for us.

As the wall started to rise, his enemies started to attack the workers, and so Nehemiah posted guards and armed the workers as well. The builders were under intense pressure; they even had to sleep in the clothes in which they worked.[89] I can hardly imagine the courage and physical strength it took to build the city wall, while fighting off armed attacks at the same time.

Later, because of these hardships, the Jews started to complain. The workers had no money to sustain themselves and their families, and they had to borrow from the money lenders to survive. When Nehemiah heard what was going on he was furious and reprimanded the local (Jewish) leaders and the money-lenders. He insisted that they stop taking advantage of the people and demanded that they cancel all debts—which they did.[90]

Because of his just leadership, the king appointed Nehemiah to be Governor of the land of Judah. As Governor, he continued to work on the wall and refused to accept the usual tax (payment) for his office. Yet the Lord blessed Nehemiah with great provision, and each day 150 people ate at his table, and he was able to provide them oxen, sheep, poultry

---

89 Nehemiah 4:1-23
90 Nehemiah 5:1-13

and wine, at his own expense.[91] Finally, the wall was finished in only 52 days,[92] but not before Nehemiah had to overcome more intrigue and treachery from his enemies.

For me, the stories of Nehemiah and Joseph (Day 29) are two of the greatest inspirational stories in the Old Testament. I am so impressed how each of these men rose from being a slave to the highest executive position in the land; how they both overcame every obstacle and discouragement they encountered; and how they never took their eyes off God and the job that they were given to do. And God went before them and provided for them in abundance with everything they needed.

I believe that God will do the same for you and me today, as long as we trust him and step out with faith and courage in whatever He has asked us to do. It's not always easy but that's when we need to lean on Him even harder. That's when we need these heros from the Bible to remind us of what God has done in the past and His promises of what is to come: our eternal reward in Heaven.

It's humbling to me to realize that Nehemiah completed his work, a massive work, in only 52 days when it has taken me more that 15 years to complete this little book. But, I console myself with the fact that I feel that "now" is the right timing for this message to be made available. As ready as I might have felt felt in the past for this work, the Lord in his wisdom chose to use a different schedule. You will find this is often the case, when following God's plan.

91   Nehemiah 5:14-19
92   Nehemiah 6:15-16

You too may have dreams or projects inspired by God that you have not completed yet. If you are in this situation, please join me in this prayer:

Lord, I ask for the faith and courage of Joseph and Nehemiah. Help me to discover the tasks that you want me to accomplish, and give me your grace and provision to complete them successfully.

Lord, help me to keep my eyes on you at all times. And to be just and fair in all my dealings with others. Help me to ignore all those who want to divert me from your work, remove any obstacles that are in my way, and encourage me to persevere until the job is done. I ask this prayer in Jesus name, Amen.

Further Meditation

Do you have God-projects that are sitting on the shelf, or stalled in other ways? Take them to the Lord in prayer, and ask Him what to do next. Then remember Nehemiah, and step out in faith.

_____

_____

_____

_____

_____

_____

_____

Revival

"When the Advocate comes, whom I will send to you from the Father—the
Spirit of truth who goes out from the Father—he will testify about me. And
you also must testify, for you have been with me from the beginning.

JOHN 15:26-27

When the day of Pentecost came, they were all together in one place. Sud-
denly a sound like the blowing of a violent wind came from heaven and
filled the whole house where they were sitting. They saw what seemed to be
tongues of fire that separated and came to rest on each of them. All of them
were filled with the Holy Spirit and began to speak in other tongues as the
Spirit enabled them.

ACTS 2:1-4

I think of revival as any new outpouring of the Holy Spirit, as
at Pentecost, and its purpose is to win new souls for God and
to renew and refresh the church. Revival is not always welcome
by all Christians though because it sometimes brings radical
changes, which can be very different compared to "normal",
"organized" church life. Manifestations such as people shaking, falling down, laughing and other "un-churchlike" behavior are often evident. Such manifestations were even evident at
Pentecost, as many witnesses thought the apostles were drunk.
This resulted in Peter addressing the crowd:

"Fellow Jews and all of you who live in Jerusalem, let me explain this to you;

listen carefully to what I say. These people are not drunk, as you suppose.

It's only nine in the morning! No, this is what was spoken by the prophet

Joel: In the last days, God says, I will pour out my Spirit on all people. Your

sons and daughters will prophesy, your young men will see visions, your

old men will dream dreams."

ACTS 2:14-17

Pentecost was of course the first great revival since Christ's resurrection.

Similar strange manifestations continued in subsequent revivals. The prayer meetings of the Quakers (1600's), Moravians (1700's) and the remarkable evangelists of the Great Awakening (1700's & 1800's) were filled with manifestations of shaking, speaking in tongues, mass conversions and miracles. The same occurred during the Azusa Street Revival of the early 1900's; this move of the Spirit birthed the Pentecostal Movement.

I have no idea why these strange manifestations accompany the strong presence of the Holy Spirit. But I know that when it happens to you it grabs your attention and you never forget the experience. Let me tell you about one occasion when I was at a Catholic conference in Steubenville, Ohio. After one of the sessions, I met with the speaker and asked him to pray over me for more of the Holy Spirit. As he stretched out his hand towards me, I felt a massive pressure pushing on my chest and I was thrust firmly backwards for several feet. When I opened my eyes, I found that I was lying on my back in the area where the band had been playing, surrounded by music stands and electrical cables; yet nothing had been knocked over or disturbed. "That's bizarre", I thought, as I sheepishly untangled myself from my surroundings. What I learned from this experience was that when God touches you—watch out! I like to think that the Holy Spirit has a sense of humour and knows just how to get my attention. It certainly worked!

I heard a similar story of a totally blind person attending a revival meeting for the first time. As she stood on the line for prayer the Holy Spirit touched her powerfully and she fell to the ground. Later, when she recovered she apologized profusely to the friend who had brought her—not realizing that the same phenomenon had happened to hundreds of other people as well.

Let's not be quick to judge as we look upon the experiences and manifestations of others. However, let's also remember that not everything we see and hear during revival meetings comes from God. Human nature and our natural inclinations being what they are, people sometimes behave badly. Perhaps these people are immature or unstable while at other times they may be under some sort of demonic oppression. We need to show some discernment in these situations; but let's not judge or shut down these manifestations unless we are quite certain that they are not from God. As the saying goes, "Let's not throw the baby out with the bathwater".

You may want to research revival for yourself, so below are a number of resources you can use; which I have found very useful.

» The *Finger of God*,[93] a DVD by Darren Wilson. Darren was raised in a very conservative Evangelical church and was totally skeptical of any talk about revival until he witnessed a miracle in his own family. Following this miracle, he had his own encounter with God, which caused him to set out on a two year journey around the world, filming the miraculous. This documentary film includes the story and interview with a young man raised from the dead, a 24/7 worship meeting in an underground church in China and numerous miracles captured on camera, as they happened. Darren has since made a number of fascinating documentaries, *Father of Lights*, *Holy Ghost*, and more. All of them can be found online.

» If you are looking for a solid historical account of Revival, all the way from Pentecost to modern times, I highly recommend a book by Fred and Sharon Wright called *Waves of Revival*.[94] This work traces the outpouring of the Holy Spirit in the early Celtic Church, the Benedictine, Dominican and Franciscan monastic movements and the great Catholic mystics such as St. Teresa of Avila and St. John of the Cross. It continues with The Reformation and into the First Great Awakening of the 17 century including the early Quakers, the Moravians, followed by evangelists such as John Wesley, George Whitfield and

---

93 Finger of God by Darren Wilson, Wanderlust productions, 2008 This DVD is available on-line at retail stores or from fingerofgodfilm.com
94 Fred and Sharon Wright, Waves of Revival, Catch The Fire Books, 2015.

Charles Finney. It covers the Azusa Street Revival in 1906, which birthed the Pentecostal movement. This was followed by the Charismatic Revival of the 1960's, which impacted most mainline churches, including the Catholic Church. He concludes in the mid 1990's with the Toronto revival.

» In 1994, the Holy Spirit fell on a small church in Ontario, Canada and the Toronto Blessing was born. If you wish to read more about this outpouring of the Holy Spirit, which continues to this day, I recommend two excellent books *Experience the Blessing*[95] and *From Here To The Nations*.[96] You can also explore this further on the Catch The Fire website.[97]

» Another book I truly enjoyed is the *Grace Outpouring*.[98] This is a more recent story of how the Holy Spirit fell with miraculous power on a small retreat centre in rural Wales. It is a remarkable story of God's love and how this love impacted the lives of those attending the centre and how it also affected the surrounding communities. It's a beautiful and inspirational story.

In his book *Heavenly Trek*,[99] Paul Cox writes:

95 John Arnott (editor), Experience The Blessings, Renew Books, 2000.
96 Jerry Steingard with John Arnott, From Here to the Nations, Catch The Fire Books, 2014.
97 The Catch The Fire church website is catchthefire.com.
98 Roy Godwin and Dave Roberts, The Grace Outpouring, David C. Cook Kingsway Communications Ltd, 2008.
99 Paul Cox, Heavenly Trek, Aslans Place Publications, 2007.

"Have you experienced God's glory? He wants us to experience the glory, and not just understand it intellectually. When we dwell in His presence, we are overcome by His power. We begin to understand that the Christian walk is not just an increasing knowledge of the Bible (although this is important!). The Christian walk is a yielding of oneself to His glory, His power, His presence! For when we abide in His glory, He is able to move on us and in our world".

Have you experienced God's glory? Even if you haven't had an experience of the magnitude described above, you may still have experienced His Glory in a gentler way. For example, even after an amazing demonstration of His power, God showed himself to Elijah as a gentle breeze.[100] What's important is not the manifestation; it's God himself and His glory that accompanies it.

Let's pray that we are all revived by a fresh outpouring of the Holy Spirit.

Holy Spirit, we wait in joyful hope to enjoy your supernatural touch. Let your presence rest upon us, we hunger and thirst for you. Let the fire of Your Glory fall afresh on us! Let your glory be made manifest in our lives and in the world Come renew us and revive us. Show us your power, your presence, your glory. Come Holy Spirit, Come in power and Glory!

---

100 1 Kings 19:11-12

Further Meditation

Can you recall a supernatural experience of God's presence in your life? If so, share it with someone... share His Glory!

_____

_____

_____

_____

_____

_____

_____

_____

_____

_____

Write your own prayer asking for more of His presence....

_____

_____

_____

_____

_____

_____

_____

_____

_____

_____

_____

United in Christ

"A new command I give you: Love one another. As I have loved you, so you must love one another. By this everyone will know that you are my disciples, if you love one another."

JOHN 13:34-35

My prayer is not for them alone. I pray also for those who will believe in me through their message, that all of them may be one, Father, just as you are in me and I am in you. May they also be in us so that the world may believe that you have sent me. I have given them the glory that you gave me, that they may be one as we are one—I in them and you in me—so that they may be brought to complete unity. Then the world will know that you sent me and have loved them even as you have loved me.

JOHN 12:20-23

The scripture above makes it plain that Christ's intention was to found one Church, one Body, and yet today we have thousands of denominations, many of which hardly speak with each other. Surely this is not God's plan for His Church. I'm not going to debate the history and theology as to who is right and who is wrong; rather I'll simply share my story—and some heartening examples of growing Christian Unity over the years.

I was brought up in the Catholic faith in England and was taught that the Protestant Reformation was about Henry

VIII wanting to divorce Catherine of Aragon to marry Anne
Boleyn. In addition, the English Crown wanted to plunder the
lands and wealth of the Catholic Church. All this is true, but it
is only one side of the story. It totally leaves out Luther and his
complaints against some of the teachings and practices of the
Roman Catholic Church; these he posted on the door of All
Saints Church in Wittenberg in October of 1571. Growing up
with only a partial understanding of the situation, I concluded
that Protestants were wrong and their salvation in doubt. Now
that I am in a non-denominational church, I hear Protestants
say that they were raised to believe that Catholics are not saved.
I chuckle when I hear this, and assure them that I was saved
and baptized in the Holy Spirit in the Catholic Church.

It wasn't until my early 30's and my involvement with the
Cursillo movement[101] that I started to dialogue and become
friends with Protestant men and women; first at the Catholic
weekends in which Protestants were freely invited, and later
as a member of an interdenominational team. It was at these
latter events that I finally appreciated the deep faith in God
(Father, Son and Holy Spirit) that we shared in common. The
beliefs we had in common far-outweighed our differences, and
as long as we respected our distinctions, we were able to be in
unity together—just as Jesus prayed in John chapter 12 above.

This was confirmed for me in the mid 1990's when, as
a Catholic, I attended revival meetings at Catch The Fire
church. I remember how during conferences, on a Sunday
morning, we Catholics were invited into a separate space to

---

101 Cursillo movement see Day 15.

celebrate Mass, which would be conducted by one of the several Catholic priests, who regularly attended from Ottawa or the United States. These were marvelous celebrations as we sang together in the Spirit, shared prophetic words, and celebrated the Eucharist.[102] I particularly remember one occasion when a visiting speaker had said something critical against the Catholic Church. John Arnott, at that time Senior Pastor of Catch The Fire, came into the room and apologized profusely for what had been said; and explained that this was not the practice in this church. That was a deeply moving and significant moment for me, and a sign of how Christian unity should work. In Day 35, I share how, while still a Catholic I was welcomed with open arms to join the Healing Rooms prayer team at Catch The Fire, another sign of Christians working together in unity.

You may be wondering why I left the Catholic Church to join Catch The Fire church. It was not an easy or sudden decision, but as I look back on this now I can see that God was guiding me. For several years, in the late 1990's, I was active in both the Catholic Church and at Catch The Fire. Later, I was invited to join another church, and as I prayed to discern God's plan in this matter I sensed that the Lord was releasing me to make the move. I remember saying to God that all I wanted was to grow closer to Him, and that if He did not want me to change churches I would gladly stay where I was. He has never challenged me on my decision, and at this time

---

102 Catholic Doctrine does not allow sharing a common Eucharist with non-Catholic people. Catechism of the Catholic Church, 1994, paragraphs 1400, 1413.

I remain at Catch The Fire where I am involved in various ministries within and outside my church community.

Over the last 30 years there has been steady progress on the issue of Christian unity. For example, The World Council of Churches,[103] which includes over 350 member churches around the world, has been working to promote this cause. In part, their mission statement reads, *"The world Council of Churches is a community of churches on the way to visible unity in one faith and one Eucharistic fellowship, expressed in worship and in common life in Christ. It seeks to advance towards this unity, as Jesus prayed for his followers, 'so that the world may believe'"* (John 17:21).

One important sign of this ongoing respect and coopera-tion between churches is the 1999 Joint Declaration between The Vatican and the Lutheran Church on the Doctrine of Justi-fication.[104] You can read the full text of this online but I include the following extract, which may surprise many of you:

"15 ... Together we confess: By grace alone, in faith in Christ's saving work and not because of any merit on our part, we are accepted by God and receive the Holy Spirit, who renews our hearts while equipping and calling us to good works. All people are called by God to salvation in Christ. Through Christ alone are we justified, when we receive this salvation in faith. Faith is itself God's gift through the Holy Spirit who works through word and sacrament in the community of believers and who, at the same time, leads believers into that renewal of life which God will bring to completion in eternal life."

103 World Council of Churches website is oikoumene.org

104 http://vatican.va/roman_curia/pontifical_councils/chrstuni/documents/
     rc_pc_chrstuni_doc_31101999_cath-luth-joint-declaration_en.html

Another organization, made up of Catholics and Evangelicals, working in unity together is called "United in Christ".[105] Their mission in part states, *"The mission of United in Christ is to promote the reconciliation of all Christians and Christian churches who profess Jesus Christ as Lord and Messiah through worship, prayer, preaching, teaching, and interdenominational fellowship and to promote the Christian religion. These truths are lived out through the power and the gifts of the Holy Spirit emanating from a personal relationship with Jesus Christ. Therefore, let there be unity in what is necessary, freedom in what is unsettled and in all things charity".*

A major breakthrough occurred in February 2014 through a video communication between Pope Francis and Kenneth Copeland (Founder of KCM Ministries).[106] In the video Pope Francis makes a heartfelt cry for Christian unity based upon "reconciled diversity." By this statement he means being reconciled as fellow Christians while respecting our denominational differences. Following this video, there was a follow-up meeting in June 2014 in The Vatican between The Pope, Kenneth Copeland, James Robison (Founder of Life Outreach Int.), Geoff Tunnicliffe (Head of Worldwide Evangelical Alliance) and other Evangelical leaders including John and Carol Arnott (Founding Pastors of Catch The Fire). This was a highly successful meeting and discussions continue to improve understanding and cooperation between churches. One sign of this understanding and cooperation was the presence of

105 United in Christ website is united-in-christ.com
106 Pope to Copeland:Catholics and Charismatics must spiritually unite—Stand Up For The Truth.

Catholic Cardinal Collins of Toronto, speaking at a Catch The Fire conference in January 2015. At this meeting he spoke with great wisdom and humility and at the conclusion of his talk he was given a standing ovation. All of this would have been unheard of a decade ago, and bodes well for future dialogue and cooperation. Understand that Christian unity is not limited to Catholics, or Charismatics, but is God's will for all Christians everywhere in the world. I am simply sharing from my own personal experience, with these two diverse expressions of Christ's body.

I invite you to pray this prayer for Christian unity with me:

Lord Jesus we come into agreement with your desire that we all be one in you. We are sorry for our part in the continuing disunity in your Church And we ask your forgiveness. Help us to respect and dialogue with one another. Break off any false beliefs we have about each other, and show us that what we have in common far outweighs our differences.

Lord Jesus, help us focus on You. And together let us praise, worship and serve you in unity. We ask this prayer in your Holy name. Amen.

Further Meditation

What can you do to promote Christian unity?

_____

_____

_____

_____

_____

_____

_____

_____

_____

_____

_____

_____

_____

_____

_____

_____

_____

_____

_____

_____

_____

_____

_____

_____

_____

My God Who Heals

He said, "If you listen carefully to the LORD your God and do what is right

in his eyes, if you pay attention to his commands and keep all his decrees,

I will not bring on you any of the diseases I brought on the Egyptians, for I

am the LORD, who heals you."

EXODUS 15:26

Jesus went through all the towns and villages, teaching in their synagogues,

proclaiming the good news of the kingdom and healing every disease and

sickness.

MATTHEW 9:35

All four Bible books of Matthew, Mark, Luke and John contain numerous accounts of the miraculous healing miracles performed by Jesus; this has never been seriously questioned by mainline churches. Jesus also sent out the 12 disciples[107] and later 72[108] of His followers to heal the sick and cast out demons. And they came back joyfully proclaiming their success, *"The seventy-two returned with joy and said, 'Lord, even the demons submit to us in your name'" (Luke 10:17).* It is apparent that these miraculous powers were transferable and this continued throughout the book of Acts as we see the disciples exercising their healing gifts, and transferring them to others.

107 Matthew 10:1-8
108 Luke 10:1-9

So, what happened, why don't we see more healing miracles in churches today?

Well, for the first three centuries after Christ, healing and deliverance were ordinary, everyday occurrences in the Christian community. However, things began to change around the year 312 when the Roman Emperor Constantine was converted and Christianity gradually became the accepted religion throughout the Roman Empire. Because of the huge influx of new believers, many of the new church leaders were Roman officials, chosen for their administrative skills, and there developed a greater emphasis on regulations and doctrine. Healing gifts came to be seen as a sign of great holiness reserved for a chosen few, rather than being normal gifts available to all believers. As time went by only priests and bishops were allowed to heal the sick, and by the Middle Ages, in England and France, only the Monarchs were permitted to hold healing services. Then, at the time of the Protestant Reformation, the doctrine of "Cessationism" was taught in some churches. This is the belief that supernatural healing as well as other gifts of the Holy Spirit ended with the death of the last apostle—a belief that continues is some denominations today. For a full account of how these events unfolded, I recommend a book by Francis McNutt entitled *The Healing Reawakening—Reclaiming Our Lost Inheritance*.[109]

The good news is that today there is renewed interest in healing prayer. This is evident by the number of healing services, prayer groups, and Healing Centre's in many

---

109 Francis McNutt, The Healing Reawakening, Chosen Books, 2005.

denominations and countries of the world. This move of God's Spirit is touching Priests, Ministers and ordinary people, like you and me. Would you like to experience God using you to help perform one of His healing miracles? If He has placed the slightest desire in your heart, I encourage you to take action and follow His leading. Here is a story that will encourage you.

As I was about to begin a healing workshop at an Anglican church in downtown Toronto a medical doctor approached me and said he had been praying about incorporating healing prayer into his medical practice. But he had no idea how to go about it, and could I help. I suggested he stay for the workshop and then we could speak some more afterwards. I began the workshop with a brief talk about healing prayer and then asked for a volunteer to receive prayer. A lady in a wheelchair came forward suffering from severe rheumatoid arthritis; her right hand was completely closed up from the disease. As we began to pray, I notice the doctor watching intently from the front row, so I asked him to join our prayer team. He instantly dropped to his knees, cradled the lady's deformed hand in his own, and started to pray. Within a few minutes her hand slowly started to open until it was fully open and she was able to move her fingers. By this time the doctor was weeping with joy—he had witnessed, firsthand, his first healing miracle!

Over the next few readings in this devotional, I will describe three types of healing prayer; each prayer is distinct, and each addresses a different problem. These prayers are for physical healing, emotional healing, and spiritual healing and deliverance. I will also encourage you to pray for a release of God's healing gifts in your own life.

As we pray for healing, it is helpful to recognize the root cause of the sickness. How did this problem come to exist? Is it simply a physical condition, or does it also involve emotional and/or demonic issues. The answer to this question is going to affect the way we pray.

Jesus called Satan a murderer and a liar.[110] On Day 18, I discussed the "dis" words such as *dis*ease, *dis*order, *dis*comfort, *dis*cord, and so on, and explained how the root of these conditions are not from God. It's also important to realize that Satan does not play fairly with us. He uses every point of attack that he can find. These can include, among others:

» **Trauma:** this can be any physical, physiological, spiritual or emotional hurt. It can go back to the womb, or extend to the present. Abandonment, severe accidents, physical and sexual abuse are examples of trauma.

» **Habitual Behaviour (sins of addiction):** this is an area of compulsion where we begin to lose control; it seems that we just can't say no. Lying, cheating, sexual sins, or addiction to alcohol and drugs can become areas of habitual sin.

» **Occult Involvement:** this involves activities when we go seeking knowledge or power that is not from God. Sometimes we are not aware that what we are doing is wrong, but it is still an entry point and can lead to demonic influence over us.

» **Generational Effects:** this includes diseases or lifestyle

110 John 8:42-44

patterns that come down to us from previous generations. Predisposition to family traits such as: heart
conditions, diabetes, suicide, depression, anger, lust,
and alcoholism are examples of generational traits.

» **False Beliefs:** these are lies that we believe about
ourselves, others and God; these lies influence how
we think and act. Because we are not aware of our
faulty thinking, we often don't recognize how much
harm these lies are causing in our life. Lies such as
"I'm useless", "he/she doesn't love me", "God doesn't
care" etc., can have a devastating effect on our life.

Healing prayer addresses all of these situations. We allow God
to heal the hurt, and then close off the entry point to prevent
further attack.

This prayer will help you prepare to read and receive more on
this message:

*Jesus, I believe you came to heal the sick and to set the captives free,
and I believe you are the same yesterday, today and forever. You are a
good and faithful God.*

*I reject Satan and all his ways, and I place myself under your protec-
tion. Lord Jesus, help me in my time of trouble, I ask you to heal me
and deliver me from physical, emotional or spiritual disease.*

*Lord Jesus, I surrender myself to you. I want only to do your will, to
bring your grace and blessing to this broken world. Jesus, I claim the*

promise you made to all believers, that we would heal the sick and cast out evil in your holy name. Heal me, Jesus, from all lies and faulty thinking.

Fill me with your Holy Spirit, help me to always be aware of your presence and remain close to you.

Jesus, guide me as I journey with you. Reveal your healing truths to me and grant me those graces and blessings to do your will.

Father, I ask this prayer in Jesus' name. Amen.

Further Meditation

Are there any areas in your own life that need a healing touch from God?

_____

_____

_____

_____

Do you believe that He can heal them? Speak to Him about this.

_____

_____

_____

_____

Praying for Physical Healing

Jesus called his twelve disciples to Him and gave them authority to drive out impure spirits and heal every disease and sickness.

MATTHEW 10:1

These are the signs that will accompany those who believe. In my name they will drive out demons; they will speak in new tongues; ... they will lay their hands on the sick, and they will get well.

MARK 16:17 & 18

I believe that God wants to restore the practice of healing prayer to all His people and that includes you! It's a three step process; first, you have to believe that this applies to you, second, you will need some basic teaching, and finally, you will have to step out in faith and do it. In this devotional you can start the process—and get yourself thinking as a Holy Spirit empowered healer.

Let's start with an example of physical healing in which I was privileged to be a part. On this occasion, I was asked to join a prayer team to pray with a lady who was about to have colon surgery. She had a long history of sickness and her doctors had warned her that they were expecting to remove part or all of her colon. As we prayed with her, the team had a sense from the Holy Spirit, that the Lord truly wanted to heal her, so as part of the prayer we commanded the spirit of infirmity to leave and prayed for complete restoration and healing of her bowel. When the surgeon examined her prior to surgery, there was no trace of scarring, inflammation or bowel disease, and surgery was therefore not performed. In fact, her doctor reported that she had the colon of a sixteen year-old girl. Chalk one healing up to Doctor Jesus!

Does everyone receive the healing we are praying for? No, not always. But I am convinced that everyone is blessed in some way by our prayer. Who knows what God, in His perfect wisdom, wants for each person? Certainly, there can be hindrances to healing in a person's life, but God will always bless those who ask for His help. I have seen people return again and again for healing prayer, sometimes with slow improvement, and other times with immediate success. I recall a girl in a wheelchair who was severely disabled, repeatedly coming to the Healing Rooms in Toronto for prayer. She gradually improved and was finally able to get out of her chair and, with some assistance, ultimately walk. The joy on her face was too wonderful for words. I believe that each time a person returns for prayer they receive the grace to persevere, and often some degree of physical healing too.

Randy Clark has written an excellent book called *The Thrill of Victory—The Agony of Defeat*.[111] As the name implies this book includes his testimonies of miraculous healings, but also cases of apparent dismal failure. He concludes with the message that we should always press in for more, and minister with the fullness of God's love in our hearts.

---

111 Randy Clark, The Thrill of Victory—The Agony of Defeat, Global Awakening, 2009.

Of course, we can pray healing prayer for ourselves, but there seems to be special power when we pray for others. At our church's regular Sunday meeting the leaders will often ask the congregation to turn to the person sitting beside them and inquire if they need physical healing. As the church community prays for one another there have been many reports of physical healing. I have had people come up to me several weeks later to report that they are still pain free. So, as opportunity presents itself, I encourage you to pray for others. Perhaps you have a family member, friend or relative or even a pet that is sick?

I hope you are not offended with the idea of praying for a pet. Here's a story about our family pet, a cockapoo terrier, called Taffy. When Taffy was around fifteen years old, he became very sick; and our vet diagnosed a severe kidney problem and recommended surgery. At this time we could not afford the expense, we also did not want to put Taffy through the trauma of an operation at his age, so we brought him home. That evening I prayed over Taffy and from that moment he became well. He received absolutely no treatment for his kidney, and lived for another five years! I believe that God is asking us to step out in faith so that He can bless us and all those that we love. Remember, God loves the whole world and declared everything in it, good!

In my experience, there is no one method or style of healing prayer that always produces results; I believe this is because God wants us to depend on Him, not on a technique. I have learned that the mind-set of the person praying is just as important as the prayer itself. By this I mean that the prayer minister should see him/herself as a vessel or channel of God's love. We are not trying to change God's mind when we pray; He already knows what He wants to do. We are simply doing what he asked us to do, as believers, to lay hand on the sick and pray in faith for their healing.[112]

There can be issues that block our healing, and one of the most significant is unforgiveness. On Day 13, I described a man who had had his leg amputated with a sword during the Iraq war, and how he was healed of all his pain as soon as he forgave the man who had brutally assaulted him. Steve Long, in his book *My Healing Belongs to Me*,[113] tells the story of a man who came to John Arnott for healing of chronic back pain. Some fifty years earlier he was in an accident when a tractor tipped over on to him, causing severe injury. John asked him whether he could forgive the man who was driving the tractor, and he said no! So John asked him if he would reconsider giving this man a gift that he did not deserve, the gift of forgiveness, and after a moment the man said yes, he would do this. As the man forgave the driver, he was totally healed and was able to bend his back and touch his toes for the first time in fifty years. If you have pain in your body or any physical problem, you may wish to re-read Day 13 on Forgiveness. You may remember someone whom you have not forgiven. For your own sake, forgive them, or start the process of asking God to help you, if the hurt is very great.

The prayer below is a prayer of authority in which we embrace

112 Mark 16:18
113 Steve Long, My Healing Belongs to me, Catch The Fire books, 2014, page 191.

our authority in the name of Jesus and command the sickness and all its physical manifestations to leave a person with illness. In this example, I'll pray for John who is suffering from arthritis. You can modify the prayer to fit different circumstances.

Father, Son and Holy Spirit, John and I come into your healing presence today. And in faith we are asking for his healing.

Lord Jesus, you are the divine healer. Would you come now and bless John with complete freedom from arthritis.

In the name of Jesus I speak to John's joints and say be healed. All swelling go down, all stiffness be gone, all pain go. All cartilage and tissue be renewed and restored.

I speak to any spirit of arthritis and I command you to leave now, go directly to Jesus for Him to deal with you as He wishes. In the name of Jesus I break you off John, now!

Holy Spirit come with your presence now and bring peace and joy to John. Come Holy Spirit, come.

Now, be quiet for a moment and then ask the receiver how he or she is feeling and to try and move or test their joints to see if there is improvement. Physical healing often takes a little time, so if you sense that the receiver is experiencing peace or any sensation such as warmth or tingling (all good signs) then continue to pray as you are led by the Holy Spirit. Even Jesus himself sometimes had to pray more than once for a person to be healed, so there is no reason not to expect that we should keep trying as well.[114]

If the Holy Spirit leads you, you may wish to lead him in a prayer of forgiveness (Day 13).

You can also declare the statement below which is from the book, *My Healing Belongs to Me*. It's an amazingly little prayer that asks the receiver to become involved in his/her own healing, and it works! After your healing prayer, ask the receiver to say these words: *"This healing belongs to me, because of what Jesus has done. I receive my healing now"*. Again, be patient and observe what the Lord is doing. Respond and pray again as required. By the way, I highly recommend Steve Long's book; it will increase your faith in healing—guaranteed!

Finally, finish the healing prayer session with praise and thanksgiving to God; thank Him for what he has already done or what He is about to do.

As you pray for others, please remember two last points:

» Jesus is the healer—it is by His power, not ours, that healing occurs.

» Healing is a mystery. You will never have all the answers until you get to Heaven. Don't be discouraged by apparent setbacks; consider them learning opportunities. And if you are getting into things beyond your understanding or control, seek advice from a more experienced healing minister.

114 Mark 8:22-26

Further Meditation

Do you believe that God can use you to heal others? If not, why not?

_____

_____

_____

_____

_____

_____

_____

_____

_____

_____

Do you know anyone who is sick? Ask them whether you can pray for them—leave the rest up to God.

_____

_____

_____

_____

_____

_____

_____

_____

_____

_____

Healing Life's Hurts: Part I

The Lord is close to the brokenhearted *and saves those who are crushed in spirit.*

PSALM 34:18

The Spirit of the Sovereign LORD is on me, because the LORD has anointed me to proclaim good news to the poor. He has sent me to **bind up the brokenhearted***, to proclaim freedom for the captives and release from darkness for the prisoners.*

ISAIAH 61:1

There is a wonderful story that Judith MacNutt tells[115] to illustrate "healing life's hurts", or healing of the heart and emotions, as it is also known. It goes like this. A small boy was visiting a circus with his Dad when they came across a full-grown elephant which was tied to a stake by only a very thin chain around one ankle. Fearing for his safety, the boy asked the elephant trainer, "How is it that such a thin chain can hold such a large animal?" The trainer replied with a smile, "When the elephant was a baby, we used that chain to hold him, and it was sufficient. As he grew older, we kept the same chain. You see, it's not the chain that is holding the elephant, it's the memory of the chain."

---

115 Judith MacNutt, Christian Healing Ministries, School of Healing Prayer, Training video Level 1, 2000.

We are all affected by the memory of past events. Good memories produce good fruit in our lives, but negative events, particularly in our childhood, can cause great damage, lingering for our whole life. "Healing life's hurts" is simply allowing Jesus to heal us from the wounds of negative memories. Because God is the same yesterday, today and forever,[116] and is not bound by time and space as we are, we ask Him to walk back to the time when we were hurt and to free us from the effect of that hurt. We allow His love to find those places where we have been wounded, and to heal our memories and emotions. The prayer does not erase the memory but transforms the effects of that memory so that it no longer affects us in a negative way.

The scripture above speaks of God healing the brokenhearted. The Hebrew word we translate as "broken" means "to rend violently, to shatter (into a thousand pieces), to crush completely". In Greek, the word means "to bruise, crush or to drain the strength from". You may be thinking, "what causes this level of damage to a human heart?" The answer is trauma, especially in our childhood; such things as physical, mental or sexual abuse, abandonment, death or the divorce of parents, war, and rejection etc.

In a study reported in a U. S. medical journal,[117] doctors studied children from the former USSR that were adopted by U.S. citizens after the collapse of the Iron Curtain. They found that many of these children were suffering from deafness, blindness, intestinal sickness and emotional disorders. They

116 Hebrews 13:8
117 Ibid Christian Healing Ministries, Training video.

concluded that the root cause of this suffering was from trauma during their early years in the orphanage. Unfortunately we are inflicting the same trauma on a whole generation of children in the war-torn nations of the world, today. These may be extreme examples, but I believe that every one of us carries some burden of previous trauma in our lives. This trauma can manifest itself later in life in all sorts of undesirable attitudes and behaviors—affecting our physical, emotional and spiritual wellbeing.

In his book *Homecoming—Reclaiming and Healing Your Inner Child*,[118] John Bradshaw, a Christian theologian, counselor and public speaker, describes how childhood trauma can cause splintering or shattering of the human spirit. He explains how, as each person grows and develops through the various stages of live—from birth, to childhood, then adolescence and into adulthood, we need to learn skills that we carry with us to the next level. If we fail to learn what is required in each stage then we are developmentally delayed, and have to catch-up in a later stage. Our inner child becomes wounded and if this wounding is severe enough it causes splintering or fragmentation. This fragmentation is healed by us reconnecting with our shattered parts and allowing Jesus, through the Holy Spirit, to bind them back together again.

In this ministry, we simply allow the Holy Spirit to take us back to the events in our childhood where we were subjected to fear or trauma. It is, at these times, when splintering occurs. The ministry involves our present-day adult-self reconnecting and comforting our hurting inner child, and when this

118 John Bradshaw, Home Coming—Reclaiming and Healing your Inner Child, Bantam Books, 1990.

has been accomplished, taking this child to meet and connect with Jesus.

In my own case, I discovered several of these traumatized child versions of myself and had to go through this process many times, which was a wonderful and liberating experience. After I had reconnected with all my wounded parts and taken each of them to Jesus, all of us, that is my adult self and all my previously fragmented pieces, gathered together for a big celebration. It was here, in the spirit, that I saw Jesus coming to me and my broken parts and saying "I am your rock and your foundation, I will restore you and make you strong". Later, He came with what looked like a pail of super-glue and poured it over us, making us rock solid. Then He said, "I am the glue that binds you together. I have made a new foundation for you. This is the foundation to build upon for the rest of your life". I experience a new level of wholeness after this. This is healing life's hurts in action. Thank you Jesus!

In tomorrow's reading I will share more about my emotional healing and describe what a typical ministry session looks like. In preparation for this, let's pray:

Holy Spirit please come to comfort and guide me. This emotional heal-ing process is all new to me, but your word says that Jesus came to heal the broken hearted and that's enough for me.

There are some dark places in my past that You know need addressing with your healing love. With the courage and boldness that come from You, I will trust you to lead me.

And since you promise to go with me,[119] *I will trust you to lead me where I need to go.*

Lead on Lord, lead on!

Further Meditation

As you look back on your own past, are there events or trauma that need healing?

_____

_____

_____

_____

_____

_____

_____

Invite Jesus and the Holy Spirit to comfort you in these areas.

_____

_____

_____

_____

_____

_____

_____

119   Psalm 116:6; Psalm 139:23-24

Healing Life's Hurts: Part II

He heals the brokenhearted and binds up their wounds.

PSALM 147:3

Do not conform to the pattern of this world, but be transformed by the renewing of your mind. Then you will be able to test and approve what God's will is—his good, pleasing and perfect will.

ROMANS 12:2

Continuing from yesterday's reading, let me share more of my story. As I have said before, I was born in London, England in September 1939, just two weeks after the outbreak of World War II. A few days after my birth, Mom had me baptized in a local Catholic church and then the two of us boarded a long distance bus and traveled to join the rest of the family who had already been evacuated to Oxford. I was the youngest of four children. Dad was a high school science teacher and Mom was a registered nurse. She served in a military hospital, caring for injured soldiers returning from war.

In 1943, during a lull in the air raids, my family relocated from Oxford back to Ealing, a busy suburb just west of Central London. Shortly after our return, the air raids recommenced and we were in the middle of a war zone; I have very clear memories of the London Blitz. I recall standing in our back garden watching the "doodlebugs" flying overhead; this is what we called the German V2 rockets. I remember the mournful wail of air raid sirens before and after each air raid; and our whole family cramming into the small closet under the stairs, which served as our family's bomb shelter. I remember the night when a V2 rocket exploded about a mile from our home and completely destroyed a city block. At this time, Dad was teaching school by day and fighting fires by night. I can only imagine the stress that he was under.

So, my early childhood was far from ideal; in fact, as I look back now, I realize that I was deeply traumatized by the war. I believe this because of the behavioural fruit that I exhibited in my life. I sucked my thumb until I was about 6 years old and remember Mom dipping my thumb in spicy English mustard to rid me of this habit. I wet the bed at night until I was 8 or 9, and had night terrors. I would frequently shout and scream at night; this continued well into my teens. I remember one deeply embarrassing moment as a teenager when Dad and I were on a cycling holiday in Wales. We were staying in youth hostels and as I came down for breakfast one morning I heard several people asking "Who was that kid doing all the screaming last night?" I hung my head in shame, as I knew it was me.

At school, I was shy around strangers and dreaded speaking and even reading in front of my classmates. I worried about doing well and gaining the State sponsored scholarships required to continue my education. I worried about not meeting expectations from my parents and even meeting those expectations I set for myself. I had an abnormal fear of failure and hated being singled-out in any way. As a result I was always striving to be in control and to be the best.

As I learned later, all my striving was a classic example of fear-based Performance Orientation; and I carried these traits with me through most of my adult life. It wasn't until I experienced healing of own heart and emotions that I learned to let go of fear and striving, and to operate with just those gifts that God has given me. Today, I have overcome my fear of public speaking, and have conducted workshops at church conferences, I speak regularly to Christian groups, and lead a weekly Bible teaching at a Christian drop-in centre—quite a positive change from my earlier days.

What about you? Do you suffer from abnormal feelings of loss, fear, guilt, low self-esteem, rejection, or depression? Do you have undesired habits that seem to control you; such as addiction to drugs, alcohol, pornography or an eating disorder? Do you have a domineering or workaholic personality? Do you find it difficult to give or receive love? Are you frequently angry or hypercritical of others? Have you ever been physically or sexually abused, been through a painful divorce, or otherwise wounded by a close relative or friend? If you answered yes to any of the above questions, or recognize any undesirable traits in your own personality, you would almost certainly benefit from healing of heart, mind and emotions.

In the brief ministry overview below, I have outlined what a healing session might look like if you go to an established healing ministry. Be aware that there are many different forms/schools of emotional healing, so this overview is not specific to any one ministry, but is what you can generally expect. Also realize that this is a Spirit-filled ministry and there is no set format. Your ministry team will follow where the Holy Spirit leads if they're doing their job properly.

» As receiver, you will likely receive a questionnaire to complete. This may be one page or several pages long depending on the ministry you choose. The purpose is to give the team a starting point; they will ask questions if they wish more information.

» After opening prayers, the team might ask the Holy Spirit to take you to a past memory. This may not be a traumatic memory; the Holy Spirit knows the best way to proceed. There may be obstacles to healing that need to be addressed first.

» Once inside a memory, the team may simply ask Jesus to come into the memory and to heal it. You may see an image of Jesus or just sense His presence or operate in faith alone, not feeling anything.

» You may identify a lie that Satan has implanted in your mind about a person or event; if this is the case, Jesus may give you the truth directly or He may give it to a member of the ministry team. Perhaps you will recall a scripture that speaks directly into the lie. You may be led to repent for some past action, or you may need to forgive someone.

» I can assure you that this is a peaceful and wonderful experience. There is absolutely nothing to fear—and the resulting freedom will be life-changing.

» In some cases, such as addiction to drugs or alcohol, you may be suffering from physical, emotional and spiritual damage. In this case, your team will likely

pray for all three conditions, or recommend further
ministry.

In the section called "Suggestions for Further Reading" at the
end of this devotional, you will find books and other resources
where you can learn more about healing life's hurts for yourself. If you are suffering from any physical, emotional or
spiritual problems that are not responding to the treatments
recommended, I suggest you consult your local church to see
if they have any specific recommendations, or go online and
search for Christian healing ministries. Make sure to check
the "Statement of Faith" and any personal endorsements from
people for any ministry you find online, to ensure their beliefs
and practices line up with scripture.

1. The following are well established ministries:
   » Christian Healing Ministries: christianhealing
     min.org
   » International Healing Rooms: healingrooms.com
   » Restoring The Foundations: rtfi.org
   » Bethel's SOZO Ministry (SOZO in Greek means
     "saved, healed, delivered"): bethelsozo.com

Let's pray:

*Lord, you know my needs. You see where I have been wounded in the
past, and how these past hurts are affecting me today.*

Lord Jesus, I come to you for healing and restoration, I ask you to bring your peace and presence into these situations, and to heal my heart, mind and emotions.

If I need further ministry, show me what steps to take to seek help, lead me in my search, and give me the grace to persevere until I am totally healed. I ask this prayer in Jesus' name, Amen

Further Meditation

Did you recognise any trauma or undesirable traits in your personality?

_____

_____

_____

_____

_____

_____

_____

What action can you take to receive God's healing?

_____

_____

_____

_____

_____

_____

Renouncing the Occult: Deliverance

Do not turn to mediums or seek out fortune tellers, for you will be defiled by them. I am the Lord your God.

LEVITICUS 19:31

… I do not want you to be participants with demons. You cannot drink the cup of the Lord and the cup of demons too; you cannot have a part in both the Lord's table and the table of demons.

1 CORINTHIANS 10:21

One of my earliest experiences of confronting an evil spirit occurred in a church. My team and I were praying for people for the Baptism in the Holy Spirit, when a sweet-looking gray-haired lady came forward. As I anointed her on the forehead her countenance suddenly changed. She became angry, her voice changed to a low growl and she started to curse and use obscene language. As you can imagine, this was totally unexpected and we quickly ushered her to a separate room to pray for her in private. We prayed for the release of this evil spirit and she soon became calm. By the end of the evening, she was gloriously happy and her face glowed with the presence of God. Later, she explained that as we prayed for her she had a vision of Jesus and He embraced her and told her how much He loved her—and the demon left.

I still have many unanswered questions about this incident. Did she know she had an evil spirit before she came for prayer? Where did it come from? Will it come back? Today, I would spend time with her to find the answers to these questions, but at the time I knew little about deliverance and so I did not follow up with her. However, this was a significant wake-up call for me and this experience was largely responsible for leading me into the healing and deliverance ministry.

The following is another deliverance story that presented itself at our local Healing Rooms. A young man came in showing signs of demonization; by that I mean that as soon as we tried to anoint him he started cursing, rolling his eyes uncontrollably and speaking in multiple voices. It was not a pretty sight. As we took control of the situation, we learned that he was a Christian university graduate who was very interested in gems and precious stones. It turns out that as he was exploring the Internet one day he came across a website giving instructions on how to build a gemstone altar. He followed these instructions and when his altar was complete, the website gave him a set of incantations to say. He thought this was all nonsense, but he recited the incantations anyway. Immediately, he felt a powerful evil presence come upon him, which he could not get rid of. It affected every part of his physical, emotional and spiritual life. Fortunately, he had enough sense to destroy the gemstone altar and come for help. Because the team had been trained in deliverance ministry, we were able to take authority over this spirit and get rid of it. We then directed the young man to the prayer chapel where he could rest before going home. We further advised him to stay connected to his church and our prayer ministry so that we could monitor his ongoing progress. Since demons like to work in groups, it was probable that other spirits were involved and further prayer would be needed.

As we discussed on Day 19, it is generally agreed that demons are fallen angels who, along with Lucifer, rebelled against God. Jesus had total authority over demons when He was on the earth,[120] and the good news is that demons still fear the name of Jesus when it is used by a believer today.[121] So as we step forward in faith to deliver a person from evil spirits we are doing exactly as Jesus instructed.

In his book *Defeating Dark Angels*,[122] Charles Kraft compares evil spirits to rats feeding on a garbage dump. His solution to the rat problem is not to chase away the rats, but to get rid of the garbage; then the rats will leave on their own accord. If you merely drive off the rats without removing the garbage, they will return. The garbage, of course, is our sin and also our emotional and spiritual baggage, which is addressed through physical and emotional healing, as discussed previously. You should also be aware that there is a whole hierarchy of evil spirits in the demonic realm, including guardian and blocking spirits, whose job is to guard and protect other spirits. This is why serious cases of demonic influence should be left to experienced prayer ministers.

In their book *Deliverance and Inner Healing*,[123] John and Mark

---

120 Matthew 8:31-31. Mark 1:25-26
121 Mark 16:17. Acts 16:18
122 Charles H. Kraft, Defeating Dark Angels, Servant Publications, 1992, page 120.
123 John & Mark Sanford, Deliverance & Inner Healing, Chosen Books, 1992.

Sanford describe different levels of demonic influence. These are not absolute definitions, and other authors call them by various names, but most agree that there are several levels of demonic influence. Here are four levels of demonic spirits, going from bad to worse.

1. Level 1: These demons are not usually within a person, but gather around to pester and influence them, rather like a swarm of insects buzzing around your head. When they find an open door, that is, a character flaw or opening caused by sin, they can enter to inflame and worsen the situation. An example of this is severe temptation, which was discussed in Day 19. If the pestering persists, it should be addressed through a healing session.

2. Level 2: Demons of this level are again outside a person, but they have found a way to enter at will and control a part of the person's character; rather like a puppeteer controlling the strings of a puppet. When the person is triggered in this one area, he/she has limited power to resist; addiction can fall within this category. This level of attack can be broken off using deliverance prayers, but healing prayer (to remove the garbage) should also be performed.

3. Level 3: Here the demon(s) have managed to secure a foothold and are residing inside the person, but only in a certain area. When the person is triggered in this area he/she has little or no ability to resist. The young man who built the gemstone altar is an

example of this level of demonization. This level requires a trained ministry team to get rid of the demons and should also be accompanied with more healing prayer.

4. Level 4: This is sometimes called possession and, as the name implies, is when Satan or his demons have taken complete control of a person's life. This is the type of manifestation that Hollywood often obsesses over, and is depicted in movies such as *The Exorcist*; and it is extremely rare. This level of attack should be left to the experts, not because you or I have less authority necessarily, but because these forms of possession typically develop only as a result of extreme circumstances or experiences that a person has gone through, such as satanic ritual abuse. People experiencing a Level 4 demonic attack are usually people who have experienced extreme trauma, and will be in need of a great amount of care and recovery.

As previously described, Satan does not need to totally possess a person in order to destroy his or her life. Attacking a single area is usually sufficient to distract someone from God and take their life off God's plan for them. We often refer to it as the fatal flaw. As described earlier (Day 34), Satan does not play fairly with us. He comes into our life any way he can; for example, through trauma, generational traits, and our own sin and especially through the occult. The good news is that God wishes to protect and heal us from all satanic attack; and he has given us the tools to fight this battle.

With this in mind, please read the following list and prayerfully discern any areas in which you have been involved. Some of these activities appear to be more serious than others, but as we saw with the young man and his gemstone altar, we do always not need to have sinful intentions.

Have you ever:

» Attended a séance or spiritualist meeting including fortune telling, table lifting, levitation, astral travel, or sought power that is not from God?

» Have you read Horoscopes, believed in them and acted on their suggestions?

» Sought healing through magic spells or charms?

» Been involved in New Age activities, including demonic video games, witchcraft or the use of mind controlling drugs?

» Attended witchcraft or voodoo activities?

» Been involved in any secret society or cult, including Freemasonry?

» Made a pact with Satan or been involved with satanic worship or black magic?

The prayer below is the first step to renouncing occult involvement. It is wise to sit in a quiet setting without distractions; if possible, have a prayer partner present to assist and pray with you. If after this prayer you still feel the need for further prayer, please seek help from your pastor, priest or a deliverance ministry. For more information, please refer to Day 37 for ministry opportunities, or see the section on "Suggestions for Further Reading".

Prayer of renunciation from occult involvement:

Lord God, I confess my involvement in the following occult activities...
(name them specifically)

*I forgive all those who may have influenced me to become involved in
this sin...* (name them)

*I repent for opening the door to potential satanic attack, and I repent
for all sin that I committed as a result* (name them specifically).
I ask your forgiveness, Lord.

I forgive myself for becoming involved with the kingdom of darkness.

*In the name of Jesus, I renounce and break all agreements with the evil
spirits. I take authority over the demons of* (name them ...), *and
command you to leave me now based on the finished work of Christ
on the cross. Go directly to Jesus for Him to deal with you as He will.*

*I declare that I am a child of God and no weapon formed against me
shall prosper. By your grace Lord, I am free to walk in victory.*

I pray this prayer in the name of Jesus, Amen.

Further Meditation

Do you tend to ignore Satan and his influence in your life and in the world?

_____

_____

_____

_____

_____

_____

_____

_____

_____

_____

Is that a wise idea?

_____

_____

_____

_____

_____

_____

_____

_____

_____

_____

_____

My Lord and My God

Moses said to God, "Suppose I go to the Israelites and say to them, 'The God of your fathers has sent me to you,' and they ask me, 'What is his name?' Then what shall I tell them?" God said to Moses, "I AM WHO I AM. This is what you are to say to the Israelites: 'I AM has sent me to you.'"

EXODUS 3:13-14

Let them praise the name of the LORD, for his name alone is exalted; his splendor is above the earth and the heavens.

PSALMS 148:13

As we approach the last two days of this devotional journey, let's meditate on the nature and identity of God—entering into His heart, the best we can. In tomorrow's reading we will thank Him for all that he has done for us.

On Day 8, I mentioned the importance of a name in Biblical times, and how a person's name often describes or relates to his/her character. Today, we will dig deeper into this subject by considering some of the different Biblical names for God. Did you know that there are over three hundred different names for God in the Bible, and yet all of these names are used to describe the One God? As we study the meaning of these names, we discover more and more about His character and His goodness. This leads us to honour Him and love Him even more; and we are renewed and transformed in the process.

In this meditation, I invite you to contemplate the meanings of these names and to consider what they signify to you. I have included a scripture references and encourage you to study the context in which the name is used.

Let's pray:

Lord God, open the eyes of my heart
as I meditate on your different biblical names
that describe your character and goodness.

Help me to honour you and love you, more and more.
My Lord and My God
Amen.

Yahweh, Jehovah, I Am Who Am	*Gen2:4, Ps 83:18,*
	Exod 3:14
The Alpha and Omega, the beginning and the end	*Rev 22:13*
All present, all knowing, all powerful God	*Acts 10:36*
Elohim—Mighty creator	*Gen 1:1*
El Elyon—God Most High	*Gen 14:18-20*
El Shaddai—All Powerful, All Sufficient One	*Gen 17:1*
Adonai—Master of all	*Mal 1:6*
Jehovah-Rapha—The Lord who heals	*Exod 15:26*
Jehovah-Nisi—The Lord my Banner	*Exod 17:15*
Jehovah-Shalom—The Lord of Peace	*Judges 6:24*
Jehovah-Sabaoth—The Lord of Hosts	*I Sam 1:3; 4:4*
Jehovah Raah—The Lord my Shepherd	*Ps 23:1*

Jehovah-Jireh—The Lord will Provide   *Gen 22:14*

Holy Trinity of love   *Matt 3:16-17*
Father, Son & Holy Spirit
Creator, Redeemer, Sanctifier   *Gen 1:3; Rom 3:25; John 14:25*

Everlasting Father   *Isa 9:6*
Creator of all   *Gen 1:1, 1 Pet 4:19*
Ancient of Days   *Dan 7:9*
Father of righteousness   *Jer 23:6*
The Lord my sanctifier   *Exod 31:13*
The Lord my provider   *Gen 22:14*
My Abba, Father   *Rom 8:15*

Jesus, Yeshua, The One who saves   *Mat 1:21*
Christ, The Anointed One   *John 4:25*
Immanuel, God with us   *Isa 7:14*
The Son of man   *Matt 8:20, Dan 7:13*
The Word of God   *John 1:1, Rev 1:29*
The Lamb of God   *John 1:29*
Lord of Lords   *I Tim 6:15, Rev 19:16*
King of Kings   *1 Tim 6:15, Rev 19:16*
The Bread of Life   *John 6:35*
The Way, the Truth and the Life   *John 14:6*
My Rock, my foundation,   *John 14:6*
My cornerstone   *1 Cor 10:4, Eph 2:20*
My Salvation   *Heb 5:9*
My all in all   *Col 3:11*

Holy Spirit	*Gen 1:2, John 15:26*
Breath of the Living God	*Gen 1:2; 2:7*
Teacher	*John 14:26*
Spirit of Truth	*John 14:17; 15:26*
Spirit of Adoption and Sonship	*Rom 8:15*
Spirit of Love	*1 John 4:8*
Spirit of the Father	*Gen 1:2*
Spirit of Jesus	*Rom 8:9*
Spirit of God living in me	*John 14:23*
Advocate, Helper, Counselor	*Isa 9:6; John 14:26; 16:8*
Lover of my soul	*John 16:9*
My Lord and my God	*John 20:28*

Further Meditation

What are your favourite names for God?

_____

_____

_____

_____

Why?

_____

_____

_____

_____

Psalm of Thanksgiving

Give thanks to the LORD, for he is good; his love endures forever.

1 CHRONICLES 16:34 & PSALM 107:1

I will give you thanks, for you answered me; you have become my salvation.

PSALM 118:21

We have reached Day 40 of this journey into the Father's heart; let's take time to pause and thank God for all He has done for us. I invite you to join me in this prayer.

Thank You Father for Your creation; the birds, the fishes, the animals, the sun, the sky, the mountains, the seas, for all of nature—and of course for me.

You fashioned me before the beginning of time and You breathed life into me at the exact moment in all of history; according to Your perfect plan for me.

You are awesome, O God. Your thoughts are so far above mine, Your works so marvelous to behold. Your ways are perfect Lord, even when I don't understand them or see Your hand in them.

Thank You for my birth family, for... (name your immediate birth family). *Thank You for all my uncles and aunts, for my grandparents and all past family generations. Thank You for all the blessings, graces and talents that have flowed down to me through my family line.*

Thank You for my childhood, especially for all the love that was poured into me. For the fun times, the child times, the play times. Thank You for my school days, and all my school friends.

Thank You for my spouse and children... (name them), *and for all the love You have placed in my family.*

Thank You for all my possessions, my job and my finances. I pray Lord, that none of these will ever replace You as the first priority in my life.

Thank You for the testing times too, O God, And for walking with me through the storms in my life. It is in these experiences that You teach me how to live and how to love.

Thank You for my faith in You. Thank You for Your Holy Spirit who has drawn me and led me into an ever-closer knowledge and intimacy with You.

Thank You Jesus, You came to show us the Father's love and to entrust us to the Holy Spirit. Thank You for my salvation and for dying on the cross for me. Thank You for the promise of eternal life with You.

Thank You for your Church, with all its diversity. Thank You for the friends who led me to You and have supported me in my journey. They are all images of You, Jesus.

Thank You for your love that saves, purifies, supports and encourages me to believe for the impossible, that You love me in spite of all the times I have offended you.

I'm sorry Lord, and I repent for all the times that I have offended you; For the things that I have done and the things that I have omitted to do. For all the times that I have put my will before Yours, and most especially for not loving You enough.

Thank You Lord for my life, and now, I give it all back to you, for Your glory and service, Lord. May your perfect will be done in my life and in the whole world. In Jesus name, Amen.

Further Meditation

Write your own thanksgiving psalm to thank Him for the special blessings that He has given you.

_____

_____

_____

_____

Share it with a friend.

_____

_____

_____

_____

Closing Words

So we have reached the end of this journey and I pray that your time spent in this devotional has helped you to strengthen and renew your relationship with God—Father, Son and Holy Spirit. Of course, our journey with God is not over at all, it is just beginning and will continue for the rest of our days on earth, and then for all eternity! I encourage you to actively pursue God's plan and purpose for your life, to be fully healed in body, mind and spirit, and be a channel of His grace to this hurting world.

I pray that you will choose to stay in daily conversation with Him and to journal these experiences. Check out the "Suggestions for Further Reading" section to learn more on subjects that are of interest to you. Find me online at riseupdevotional.com to read new material, or join in the conversation.

May you rise up, on eagle's wings!

Blessings,
Michael

Suggestions for Further Reading

Baptism (Anointing) of the Holy Spirit:
Randy Clark, Baptism in The Holy Spirit, Global Awakening, 1984
Francis MacNutt, Overcome by the Spirit, Chosen Books, 1990
Mark & Patti Virkler, Baptism in The Holy Spirit, Lamad Publishing, 2002
Mark Virkler, website: bornofthespirit.today

Dreams:
Steve and Dianne Bydeley, Dream Dreams, Essence Publishing, 2002
Steve and Dianne Bydeley, Dreams that heal and Counsel, Lapstone Ministries, 2004
Mark and Patty Virkler, Hear God Through Your Dreams, 2011 cwgministries.org

Forgiveness:
John and Carol Arnott, Grace and Forgiveness, Catch The Fire Books, 2015
John Kuypers, The Non Judgmental Christian, Present Living & Learning Inc. 2002

Hearing God
Mark & Patti Virkler, 4 Keys to Hearing God's Voice, Destiny

Image, 2010

Mark & Patti Virkler, Hearing God, Destiny Image, 2014

General Healing:

Randy Clark & Bill Johnson, The Essential Guide to Healing, Baker Publishing. 2011

Randy Clark & Bill Johnson, Healing Unplugged, Chosen Books. 2012

Randy Clark, Healing Ministry in Your Church—A Practical Guide to Pastors, Global Awakening, 2007

Francis MacNutt, The Healing Reawakening, Chosen Books, 2005

Francis MacNutt, Healing, Ave Maria Press, 1999

Steve Long, My Healing Belongs to Me, Catch The Fire Books, 2014

CHM website christianhealingmin.org

Global Awakening website globalawakening.com

Healing Rooms website healingrooms.com

Healing Life's Hurts:

John Bradshaw, Homecoming—Reclaiming & Healing Your Inner Child, Bantam Books 1990

John and Paula Sandford, Healing the Wounded Spirit, Transformation of the Inner Man, Victory House, 1985

Sapphire Leadership Group (Arthur Burk's ministry). Website: theslg.com

Edward Smith, Healing Life's Deepest Hurts, Regal Books, 2002

The Mind:

Dr. Caroline Leaf, Who switched off My Mind? Thomas Nelson, 2009

Joyce Myers, Battle Field of the Mind, Word Alive, 2002

The Occult, New Age and Deliverance:

Neil Anderson, The Bondage Breaker, Harvest House, 1993

Paul Cox, Come Up Higher, This Joy! Books, 2010 (Generational Healing & Deliverance)

James Goll, Deliverance from Darkness, Chosen Books 2010

Charles Kraft, Defeating Dark Angels, Dimension Books, 1992

Francis MacNutt, Deliverance from Evil Spirits, Chosen Books, 2000

Sapphire Leadership Group (Arthur Burk's ministry). Website: theslg.com

Selwyn Stevens, Unmasking Freemasons—Removing The Hoodwink, Jubilee Resources, 2007

Bishop Bob Tacky, Balanced Deliverance, BT Publishing, 2009

Other:

Canada Book of Decrees and Prophecies, V-Kol Media Ministries, 2014

Paul Cox, Heavenly Trek, Aslan's Place Publishing, 2007

Louis Everly, That Man is You, Paulist Press, 1967

Blom Marney, From the River to the Ends of the Earth, Canadian Acts News Network, 2012

Warren Rick, Purpose Driven Life, Zondervan Books, 2012

Rose Guide to the Tabernacle, Rose Publication, 2008

Prayer:

Fr. Edward Farrell, Prayer is a Hunger, Dimension Books, 1972

James Goll, The Lost Art of Practicing His Presence, Destiny Image 2005

Michel Quoist, Prayers for Life, Gill & MacMillan, 1963

Dutch Sheets, Intercessory Prayer, Regal Books, 1996

Dennis Wiedrick, A Royal Priesthood, Wiedrick & Associates, 1997

Revival:

John Arnott (general editor), Experience The Blessings, Renew Books, 2000

Roy & Roberts Dave Godwin, The Grace Outpouring, David Cook Books, 2008

Revival website, revival-library.org

Jerry Steingard with John Arnott, Catch The Fire Books, 2014

Darren Wilson, Finger of God DVD, Wonderlust Productions

Fred & Sharon Wright, Waves of Revival, Catch The Fire Books, 2015

Topical Index

Hearing God	16 (83), 17 (90), 28 (145)
Holy Spirit	3 (19), 5 (27), 15 (76), 24 (127), 32 (166)
Healing Life's Hurts	21 (110), 23 (122), 24 (127), 36 (193), 37 (198)
Jesus	2 (15), 5 (27), 8 (41), 9 (45), 10 (50), 11 (55), 15 (76)
Journaling	17 (90), 24 (127), 25 (131)
Mind Renewing	18 (95)
Occult/Deliverance	38 (204)
Perseverance	12 (60), 31 (161)
Pray (how to)	7 (35), 17 (90)
Prayers for:	
Daily Offering	7 (35)
Guidance	7 (35)
Faith	8 (41), 26 (135)
Praise	21 (110), 22 (117), 39 (212)
Prophetic Word	8 (41), 21 (110), 22 (117), 39 (212)
Salvation	6 (31)
Thanksgiving	40 (216)
Prophecy	21 (110), 22 (117)
Revival	15 (76), 32 (166)
Salvation	6 (31), 20 (105)
Satan/Devil	18 (95), 19 (99), 34 (180), 38 (204)
Temptation (overcoming)	19 (99)
Tongues (gift of)	27 (139)
Trinity (3-in-1 God)	5 (27)

Acknowledgements

They say it takes a village to raise a child; it seems to me that the same sentiment applies to writing a book. I would like to thank and acknowledge the "village" without whom this book would never have been written.

Thank you to Alwyn Almeida, the prophet who first told me that God wanted me to write a book; without his intervention I doubt that I would ever have started this project. And thanks to the amazing team, especially Jayne Carreiro and Betty Anne Cumberbatch, who helped lead and organize the School of Healing Prayer which has been foundational to many of the stories in this book.

Thanks to all my friends and mentors at Catch The Fire church, especially Pastors Steve Long and John Bootsma. These last fifteen years have been a wonderful time of experiencing God's love, and I deeply appreciate all that you and Catch The Fire have done for me.

A huge thank you to my writing guides and coaches, especially Akemi Tomoda who encouraged me to take my manuscript off the shelf and to keep working to have it published. Also to Cheryl Antao-Xavier who introduced me to the world of publishing and inspired me to keep moving forward. Many thanks to Lisa Murphy-Whate, my daughter-in-law, for her invaluable assistance in pre-editing early drafts. Thanks to Nina Munteanu, my creative writing coach, for helping me bring life into my writing and stories, and to Jim Taylor for his treasured insight and editorial comment. Finally to Jonathan Puddle, Benjamin Jackson, Marcott Bernarde and everyone else at Catch The Fire Books who transformed my final manuscript into what you are reading today.

I would like to acknowledge my family, without whom I would have no story to tell. I extend my heartfelt love and thanks to my wife Marion, my sons Steve, Rich and Rob, their wives and my seven grandchildren, whose love and support has kept me going through all the peaks and valleys of my journey.

Finally, thank you God—Father, Son and Holy Spirit—for inspiring me to write this devotional, and for guiding me every step of the way. There were certainly times when I felt like giving up, but You found ways to encourage me and gave me the grace to persevere to the end. All the honour and glory belong to you—My Lord, and My God.

YOU WERE MADE FOR MORE

A God who loves you

wants you to experience him

be transformed

and given power

At Catch The Fire, we are passionate about seeing people be transformed by a living God. We have many books that can help you on your journey, but we are also involved in much more.

Why not join us at a conference or seminar this year? Or come on a short-term mission with us? Or have your heart radically changed at a 5-month school. Or just visit one of our churches in many cities around the world.

CONTINUE YOUR JOURNEY AT

catchthefirebooks.com/whatsnext